Through Their Eyes:

Covered Bridges of Harrison County, Kentucky

Melissa C. Jurgensen

ISBN: 061569747X

ISBN-13: 978-0615697475

CONTENTS:

Note from the author:

The books in this series are not intended to be definitive histories of the bridges, however I have researched them extensively. Rather than having them sitting in a file cabinet where no one sees them, I wanted to share the photos of these wooden treasures I have collected through the years and/or been loaned by some wonderful people I have met along the way.

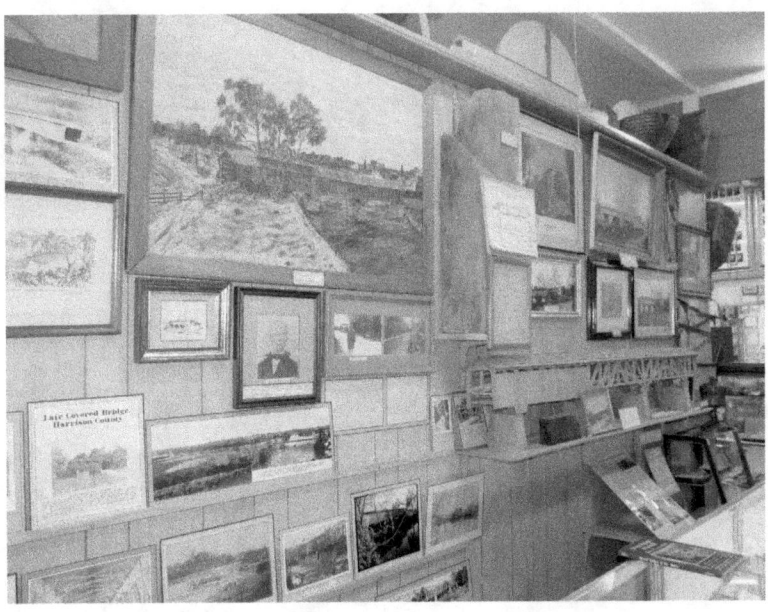

INTRODUCTION

Covered bridges were engineering accomplishments of their day. Some were built by celebrated architects while others were built by men with no formal training, just an understanding of the art form that is the covered bridge. Bridges gracefully served for many years but sometimes as they aged, with or without maintenance, many saw them as obsolete and wanted them to be replaced with more modern structures, such as concrete or iron bridges or they were lost to other unfortunate circumstances such as a fire or flood. The "Through Their Eyes" series celebrates the photographers of yesteryear who captured these structures in their photographs to preserve them for all time.

In the heart of the Bluegrass region of Kentucky, Harrison County was potentially home to up to fifteen covered bridges but sadly, none of these bridges remain today. Some have disappeared without a trace while remnants of the others have left small clues of their existence, such as abutments or a stone pier.

Through my research I have only been able to locate photos of four of the bridges of Harrison County: Claysville, Cynthiana, Lair Station and Gray's Run. Photos of the other bridges such as the Indian Creek Bridge or the Falmouth Pike Bridge have been lost to time. The photograph collection contained within these pages is intended to give a glimpse into the life span of the bridge and to an extent, the surrounding community. Whenever possible I have included personal recollections of the bridges from area locals.

Claysville

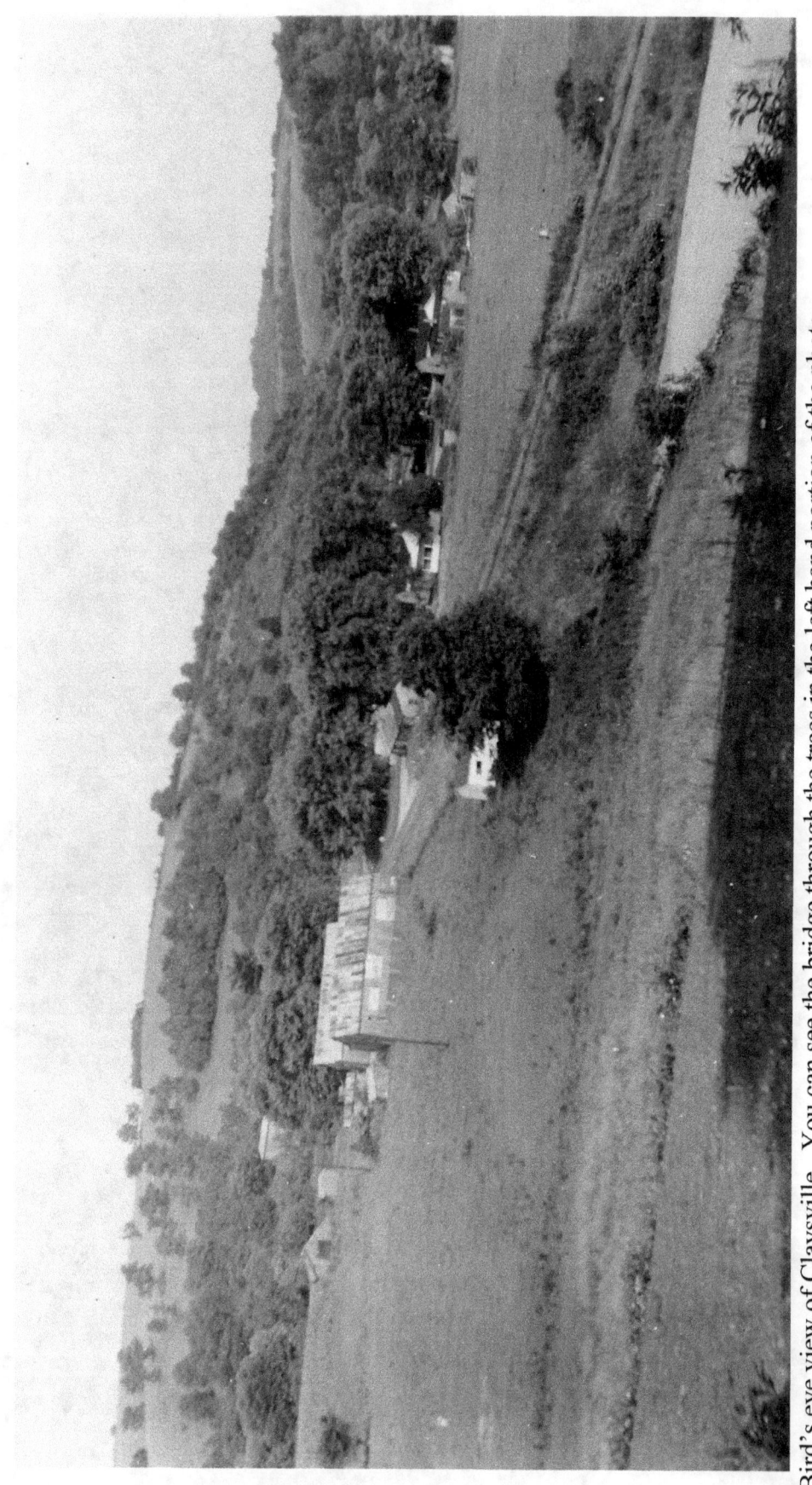

Bird's eye view of Claysville. You can see the bridge through the trees in the left hand portion of the photo.

1944

Claysville was a small community on the Harrison-Robertson County line near the mouth of Beaver Creek and the Licking River. Until 1953 it was home to the last surviving covered bridge in the county.

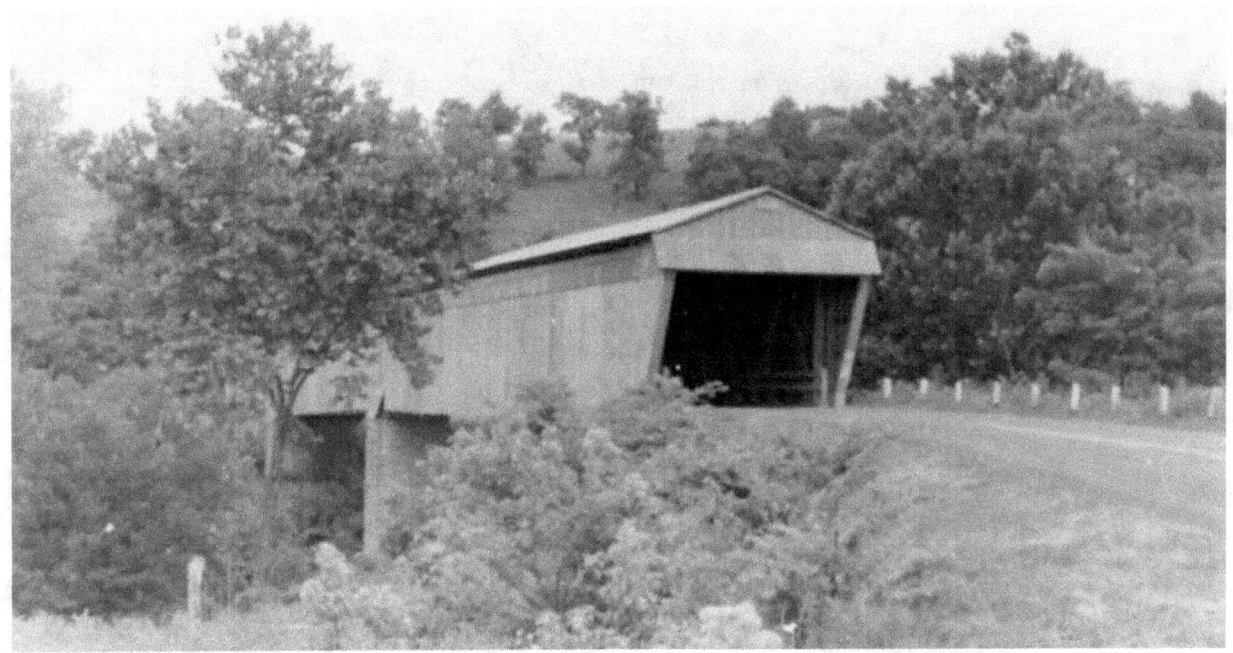

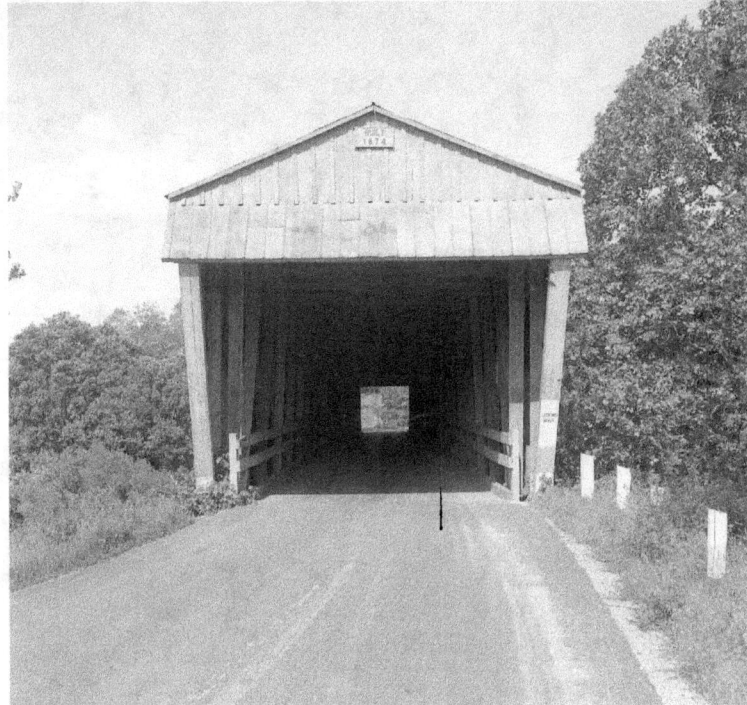

May 21, 1944

In 1874 the Bower Bridge Company was contracted to construct a covered bridge across the Licking River in Claysville. The end result was a 307 foot, two span bridge of Howe truss configuration. A ferry operated at the site in the years before the bridge was built.

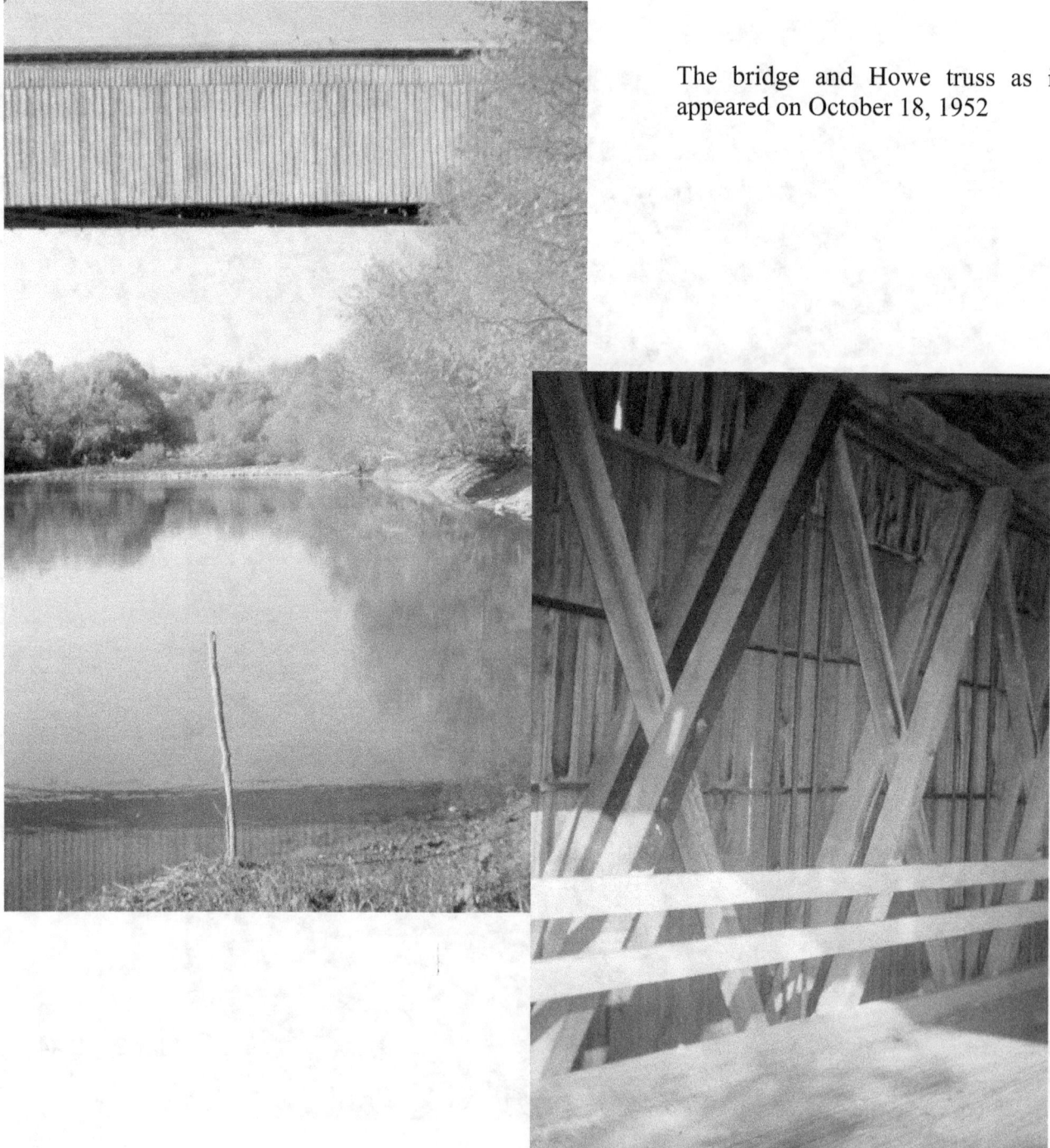

The bridge and Howe truss as it appeared on October 18, 1952

The massive structure towered nearly forty feet above the river and the two spans were joined on a massive limestone pier.

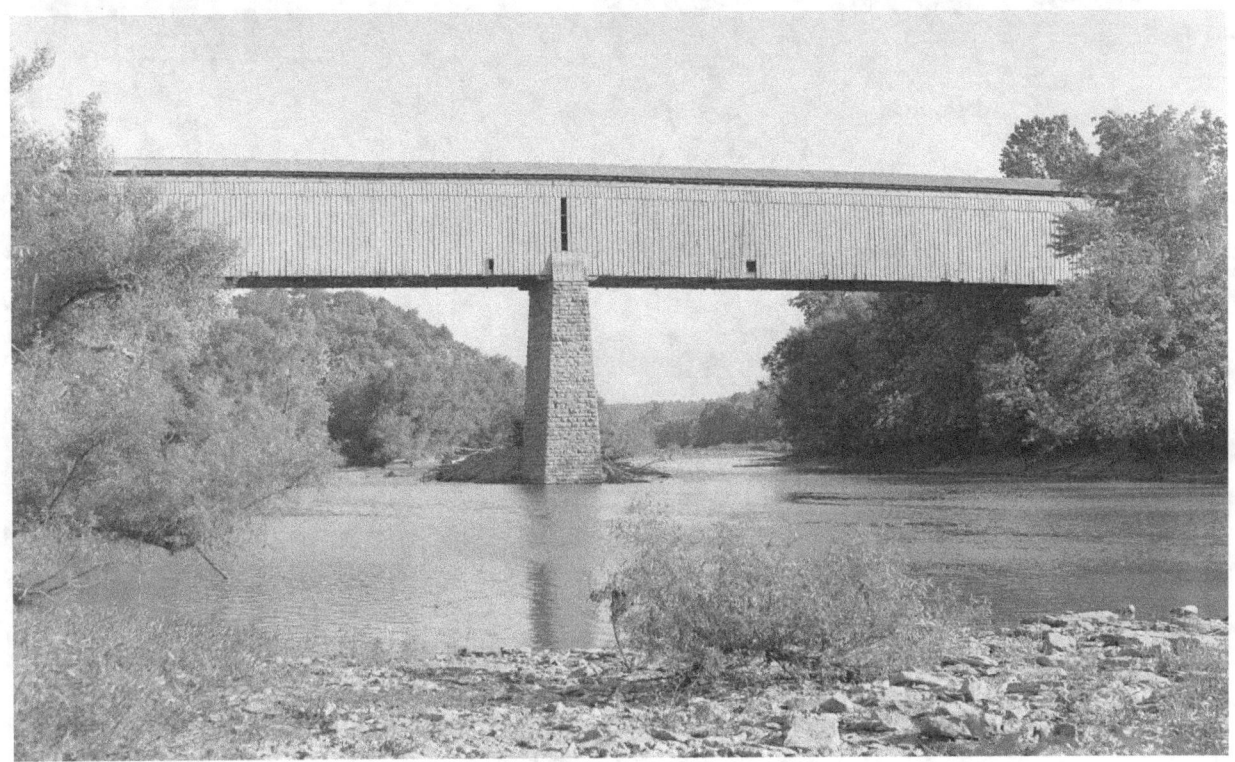

May 31, 1948

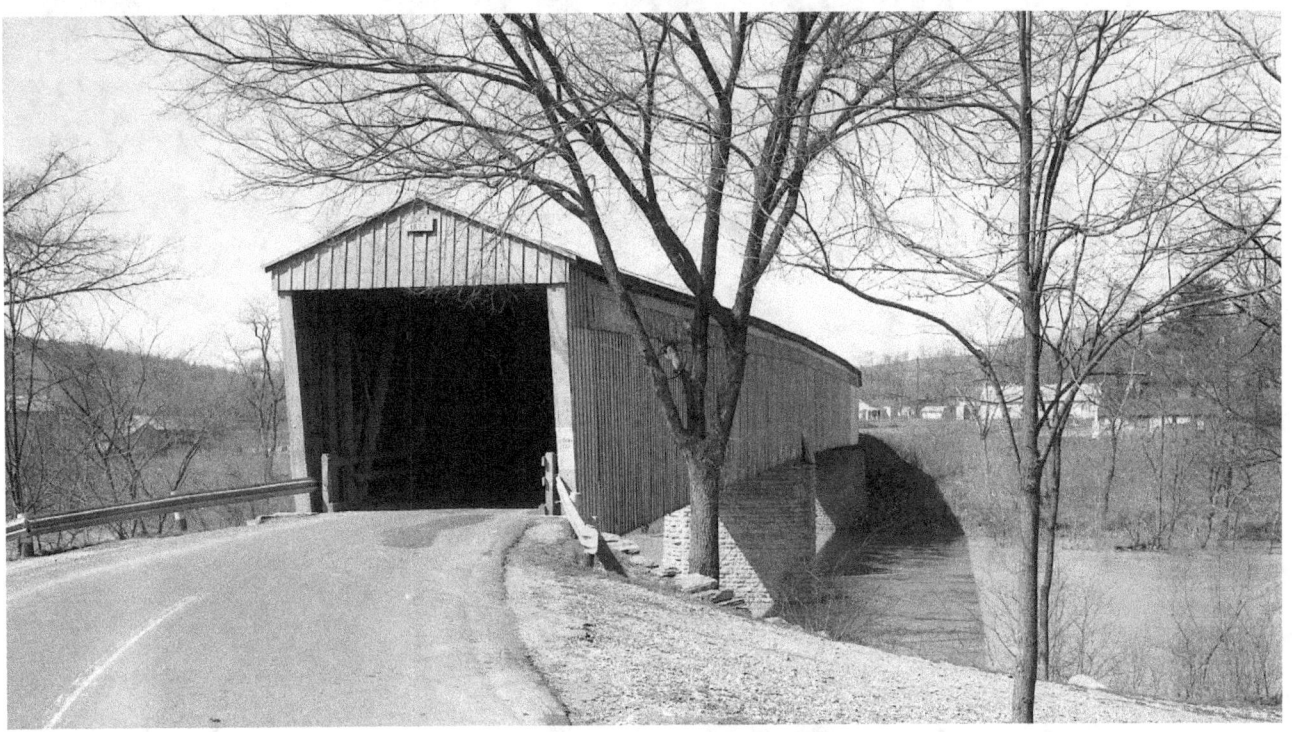

April 14, 1944

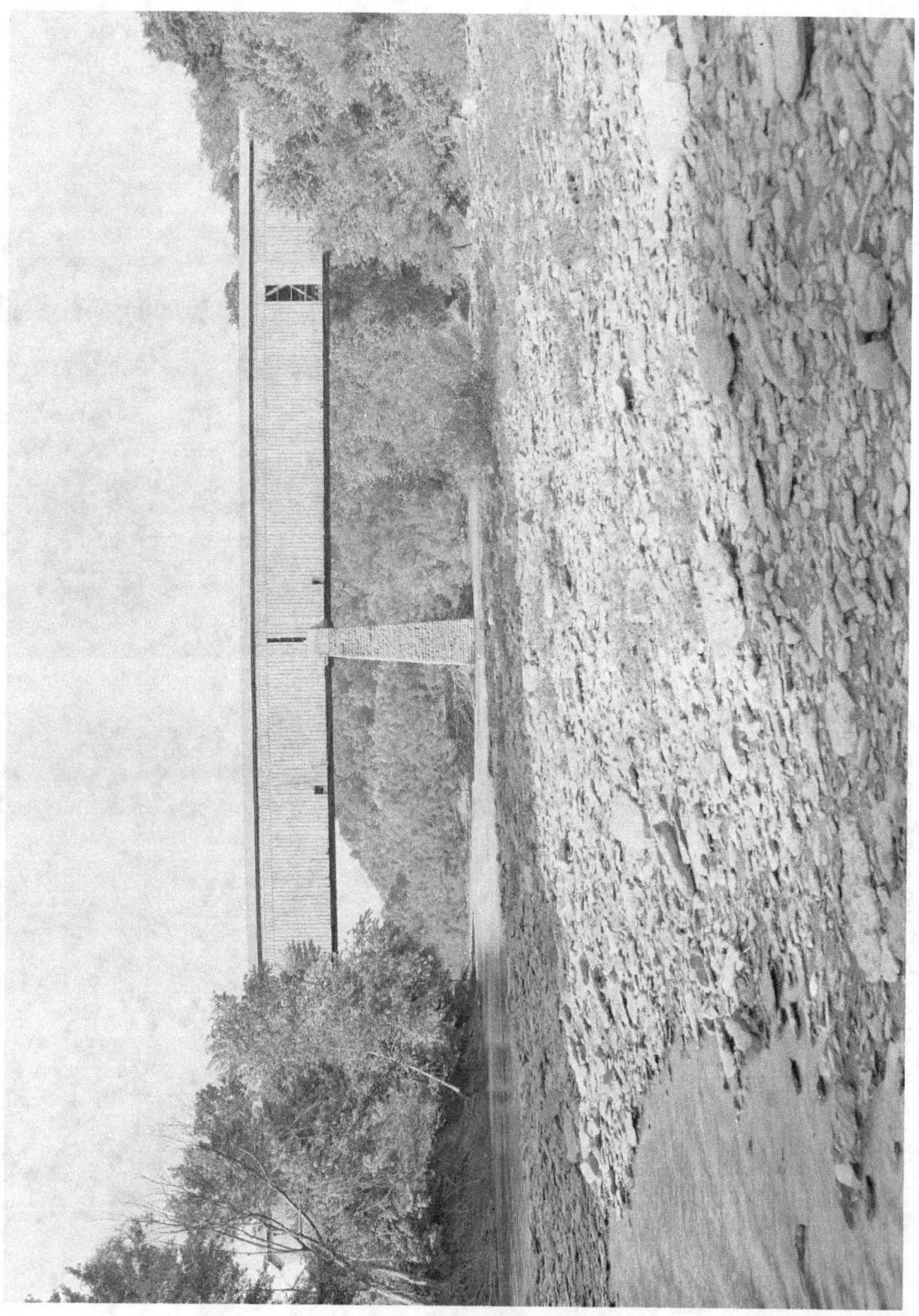

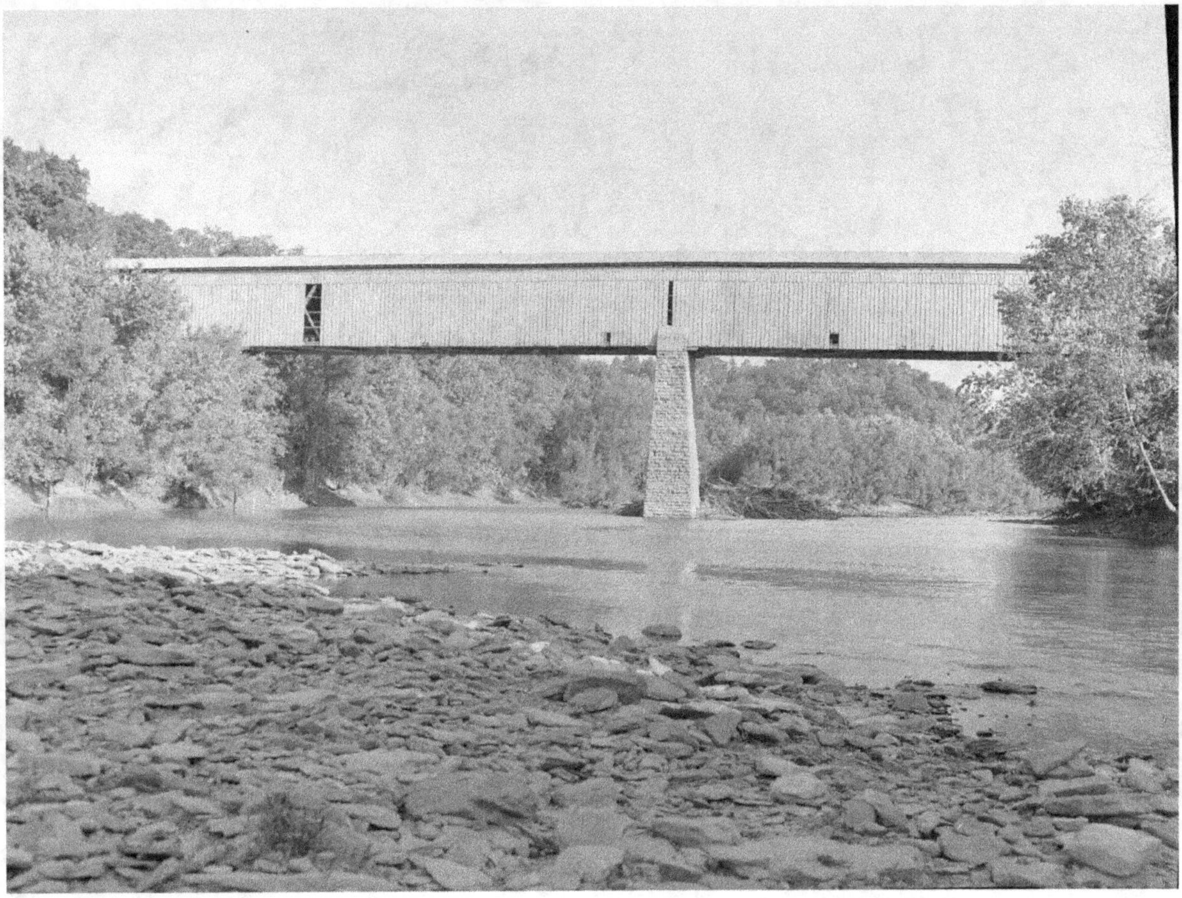

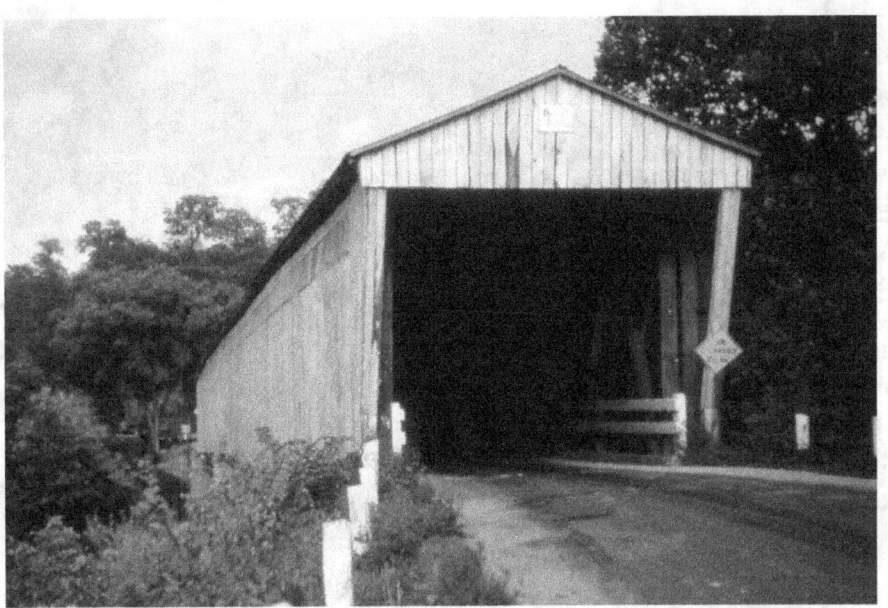

May 31, 1948

August 21, 1951

The Claysville bridge held the distinction of being the only covered bridge in Kentucky to carry a federal highway. (US 62)

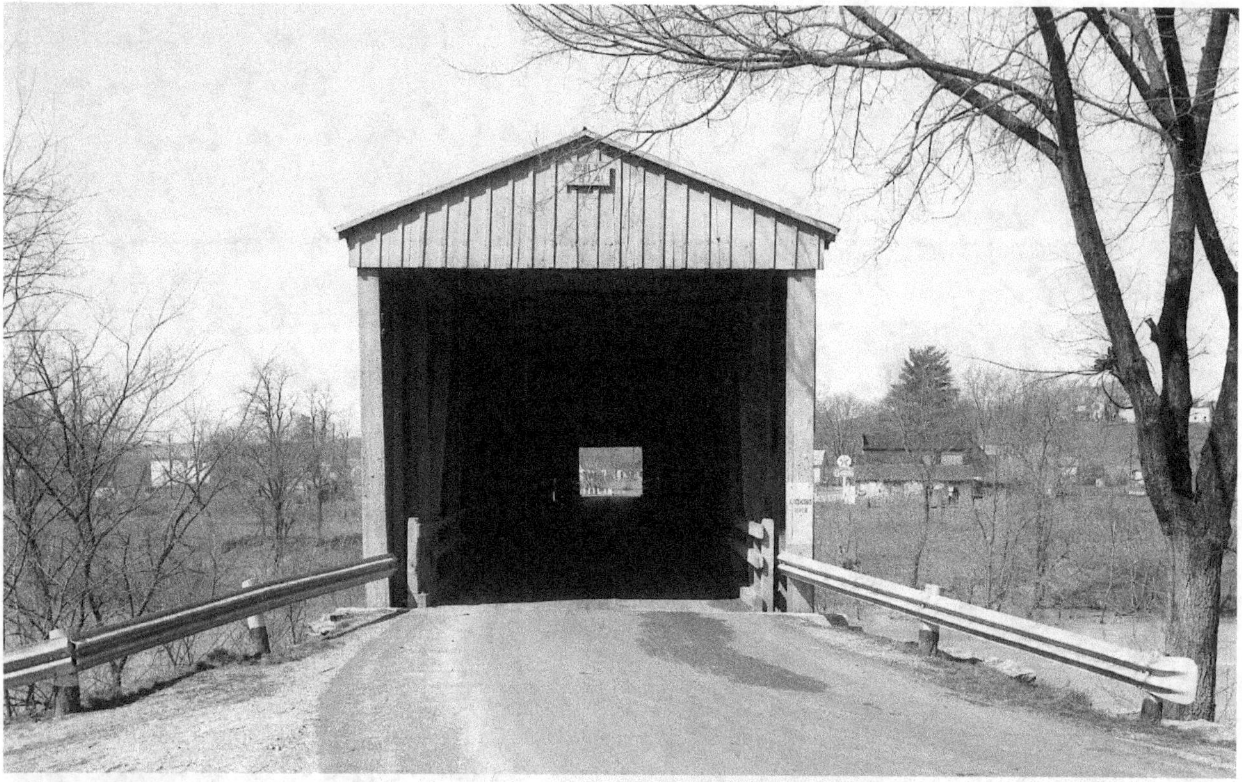

April 15, 1944

After the bridge was built, local lore tells the story of a fine being assessed upon anyone caught running their horse through the bridge. One day a local, after having visited an area tavern was seen doing so by the toll collector and was fined. The man paid a double fine to the toll collector and turned his horse around and ran it through the bridge again.

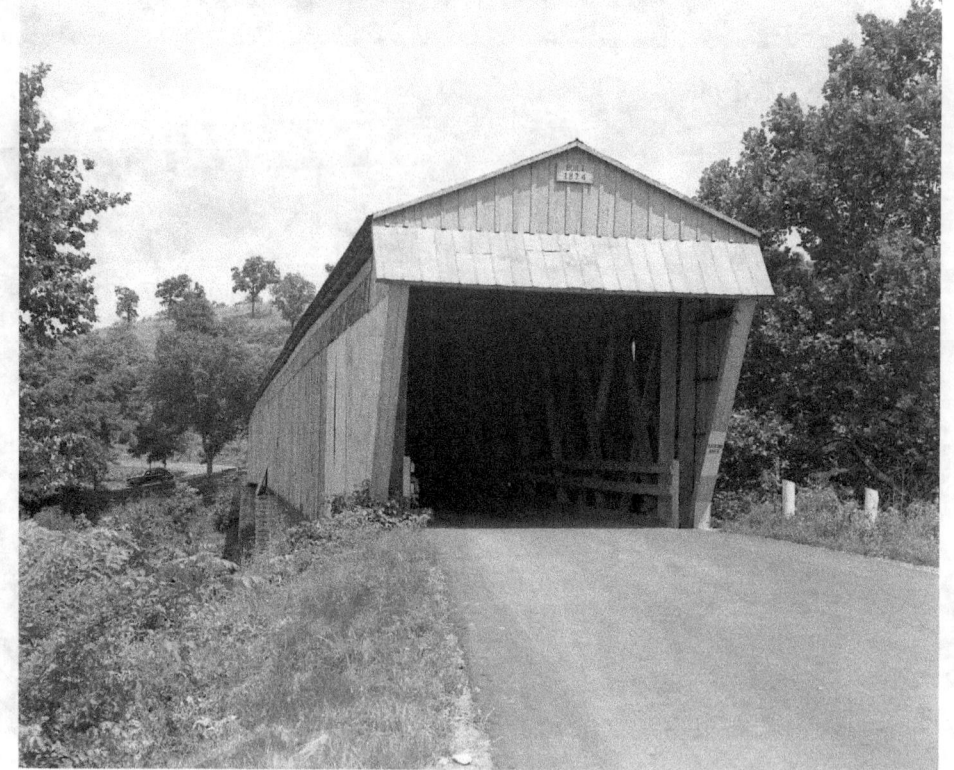

June 21 1942

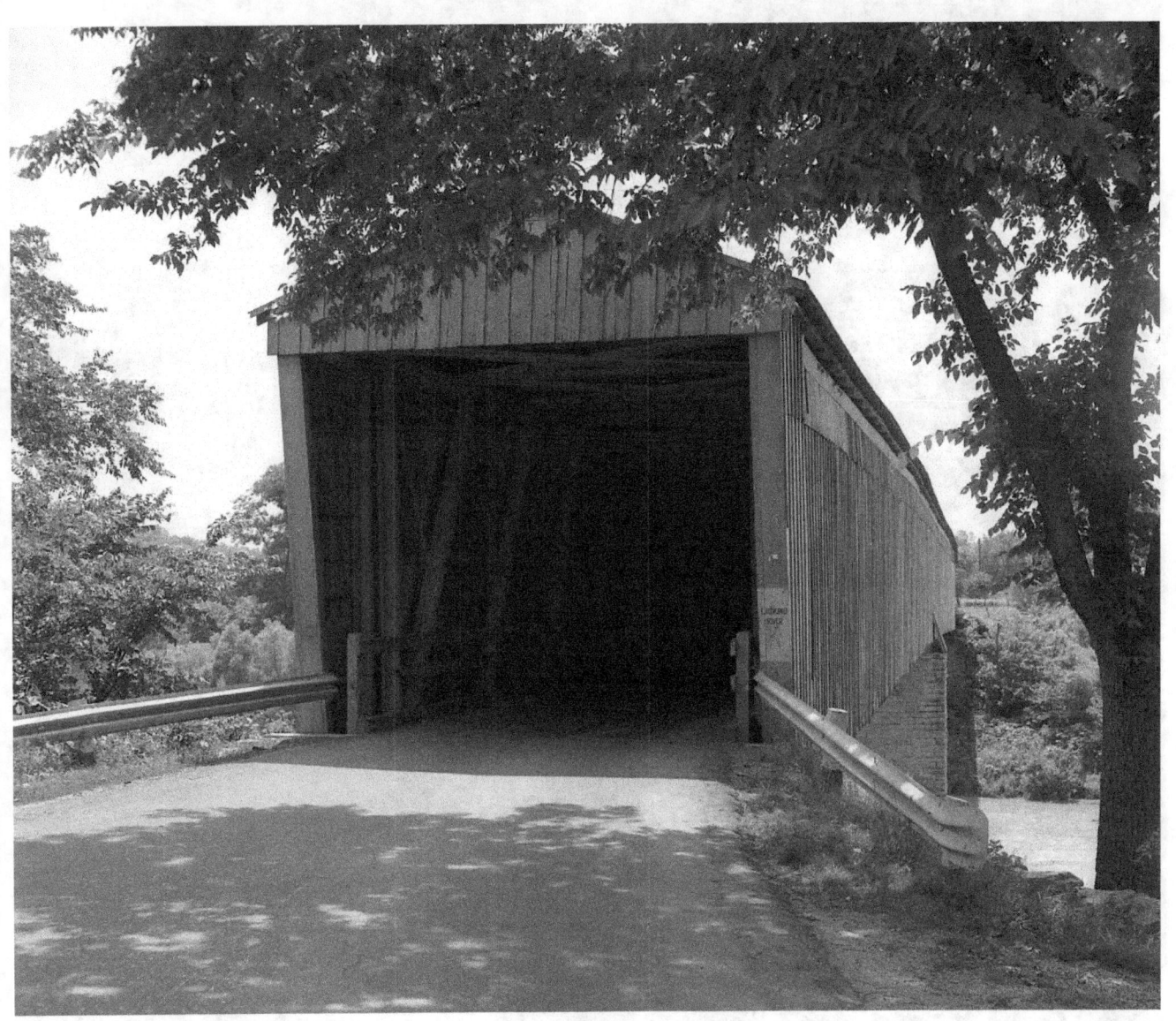

A shady summer afternoon.

June 21, 1942

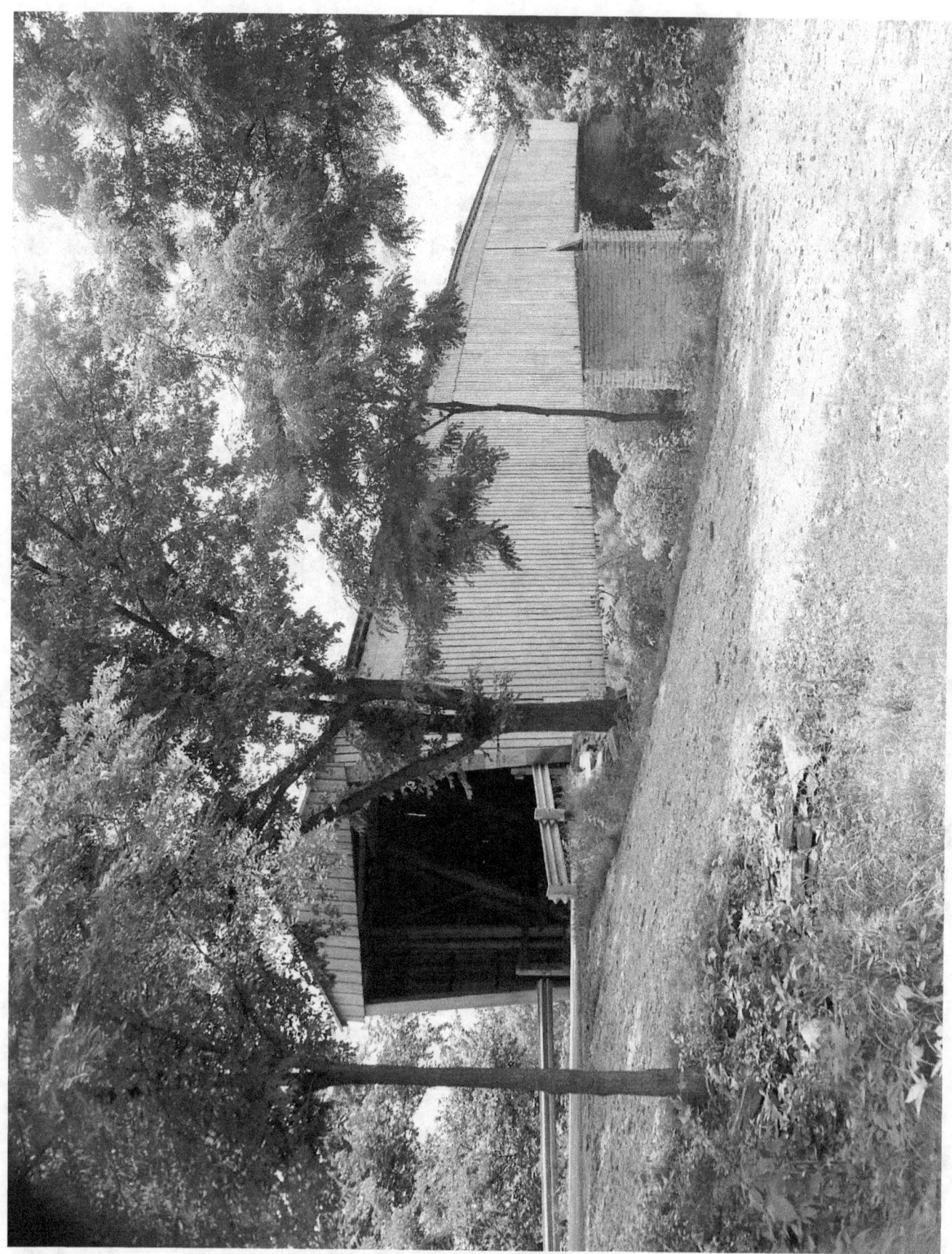

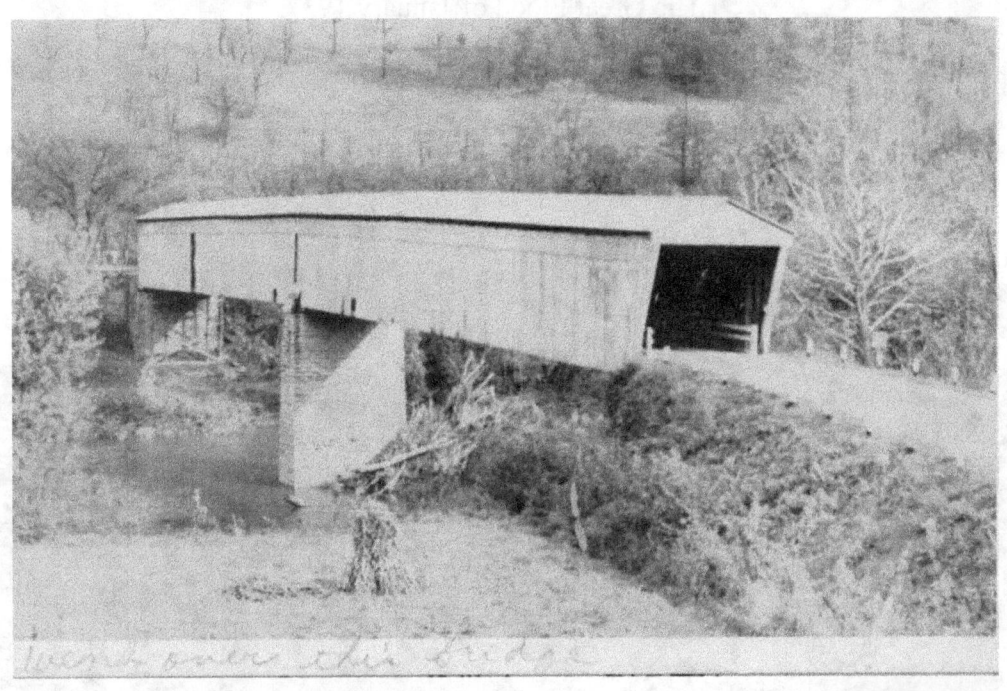

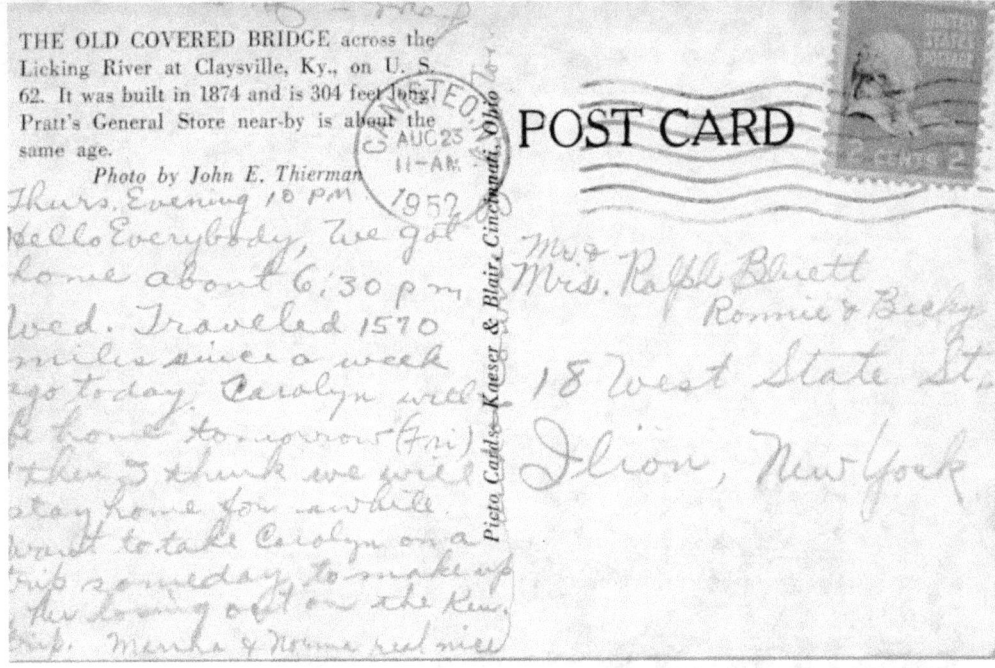

This postcard mailed on August 23, 1952 has "Went over this bridge" noted on the front and an eye catching line on the back of the postcard states "Traveled 1570 miles since a week ago today." That was quite a trip!

The Great Flood of January 1937.

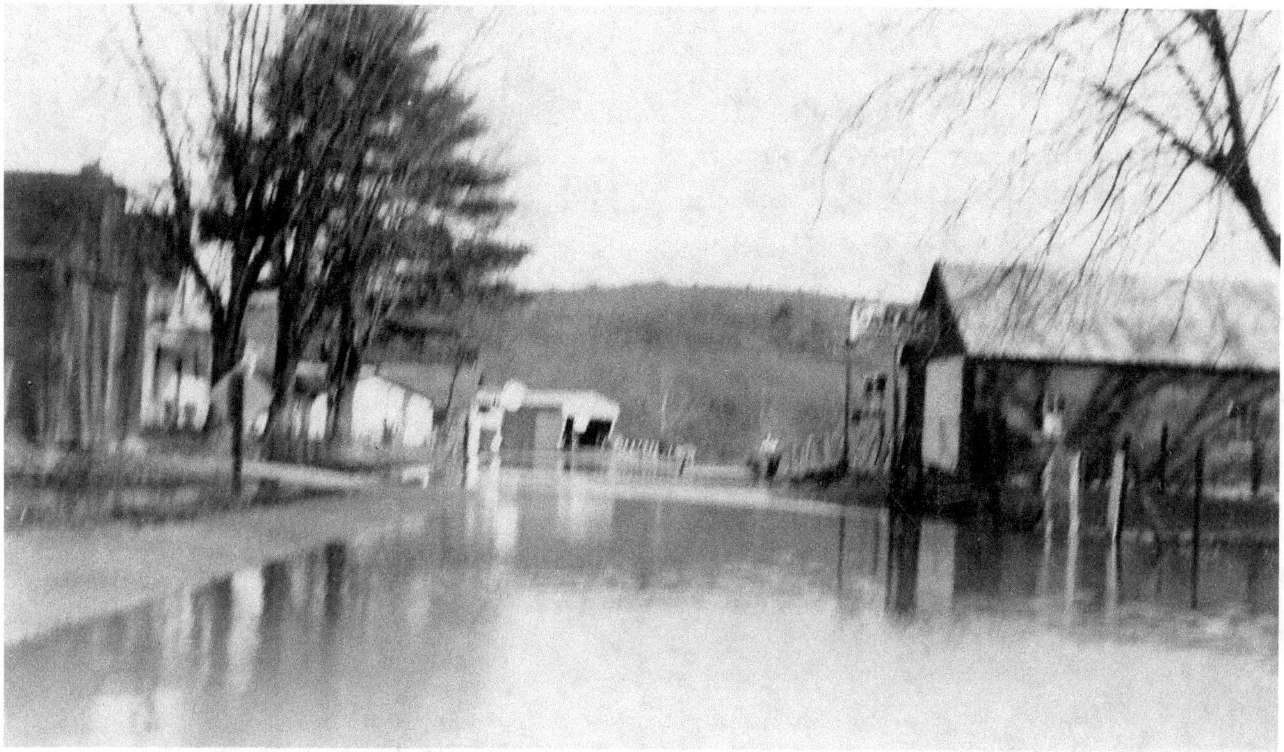

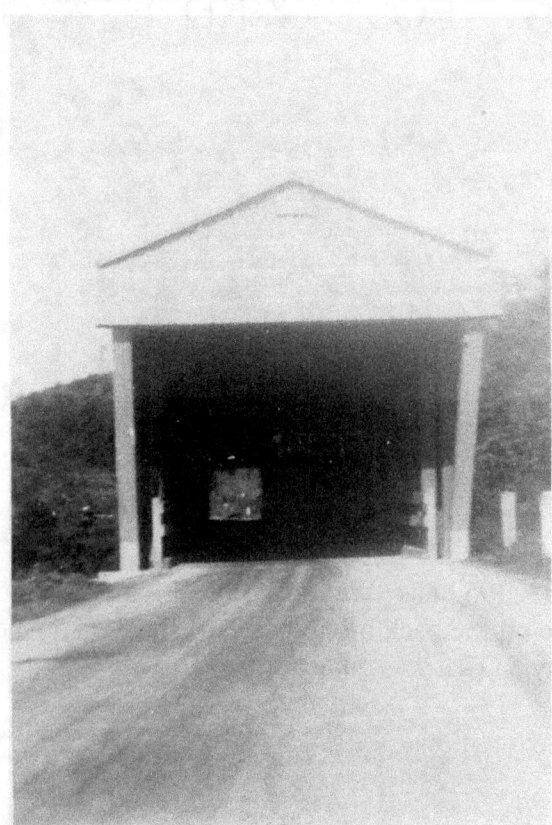

1938

Forrest B. Thompson operated a general store on the Harrison County side of the bridge from 1932 until he sold the business in November of 1948 upon his retirement. The Thompson family lived in a home that was attached to the general store.

1940

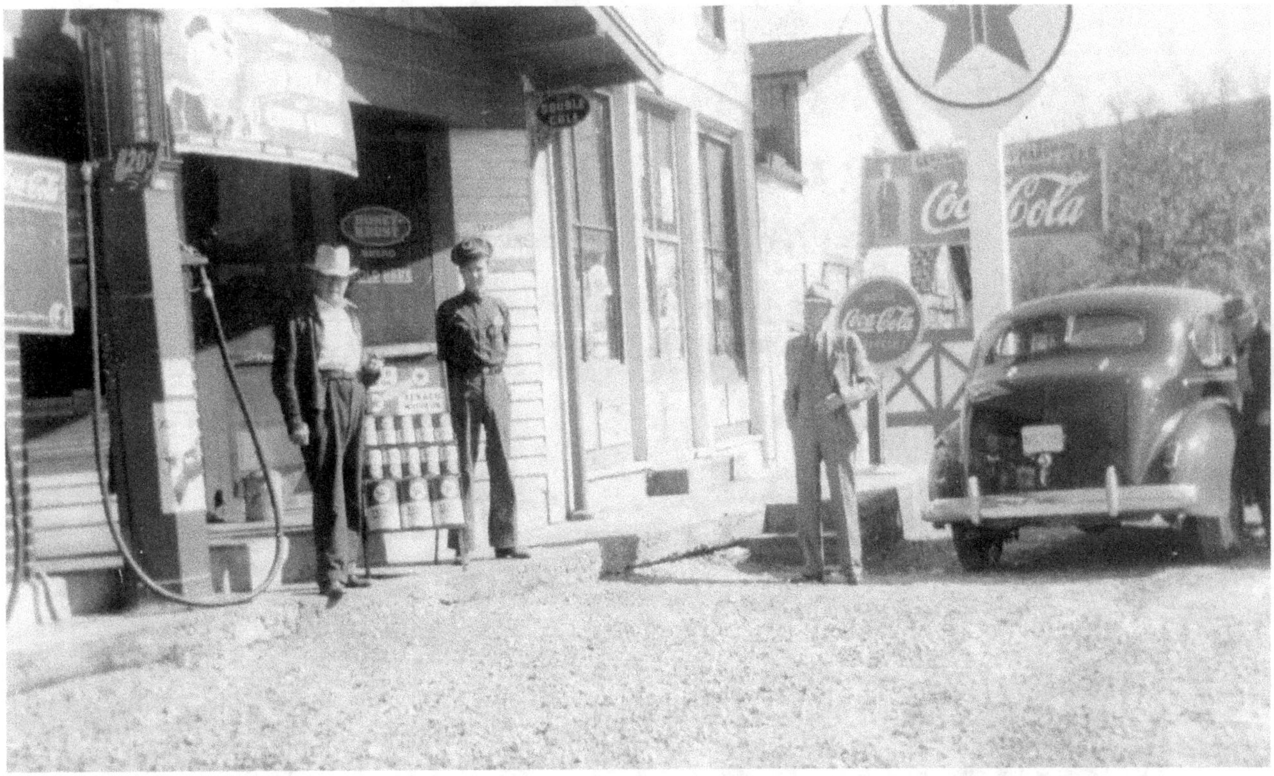

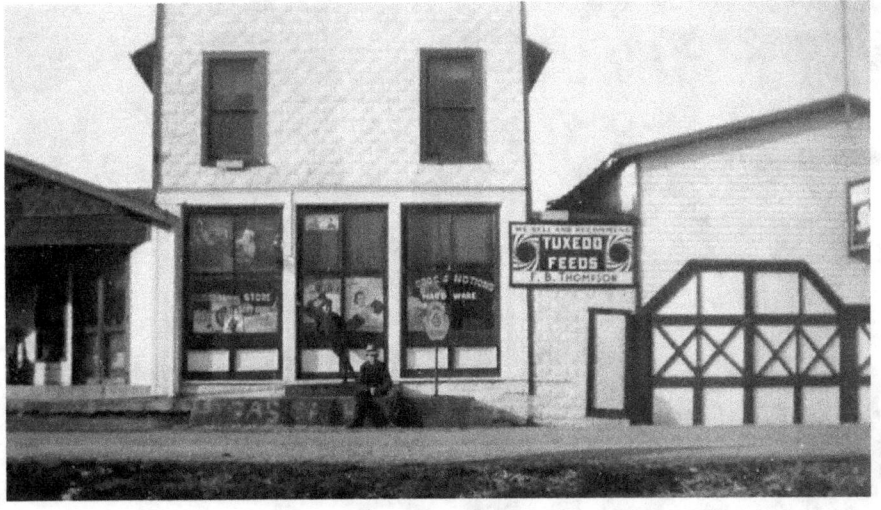

The General Store, supplied locals as well as travelers with a place to stop for refreshments, gas, groceries, hardware and even livestock feed.

1936

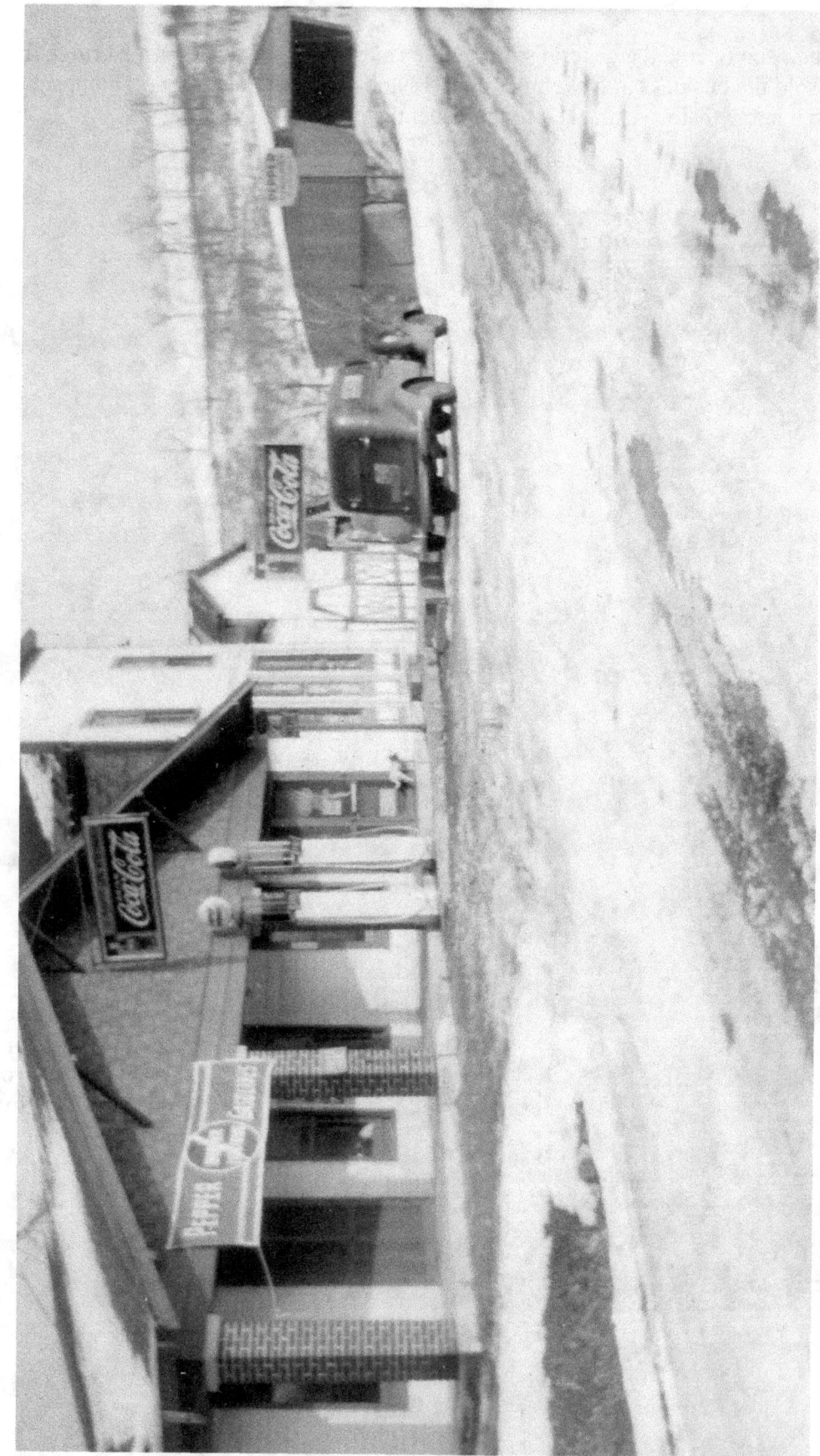

1939

22

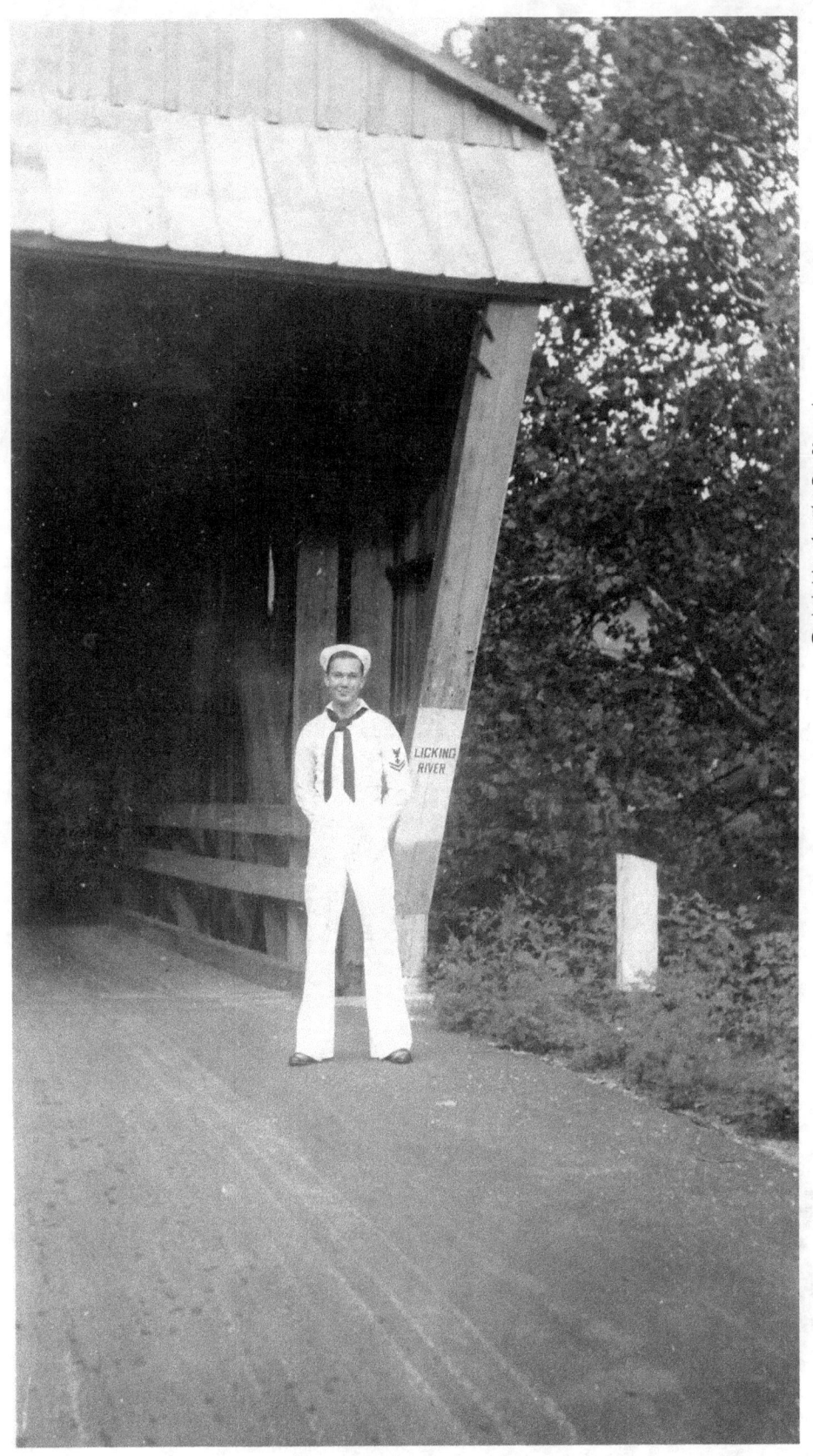

William (Bill) Thompson assisted his father in the daily operation of the store until it closed. However, he was absent during his service in the US Navy as a Pharmacist's Mate, First Class during WWII.

1944

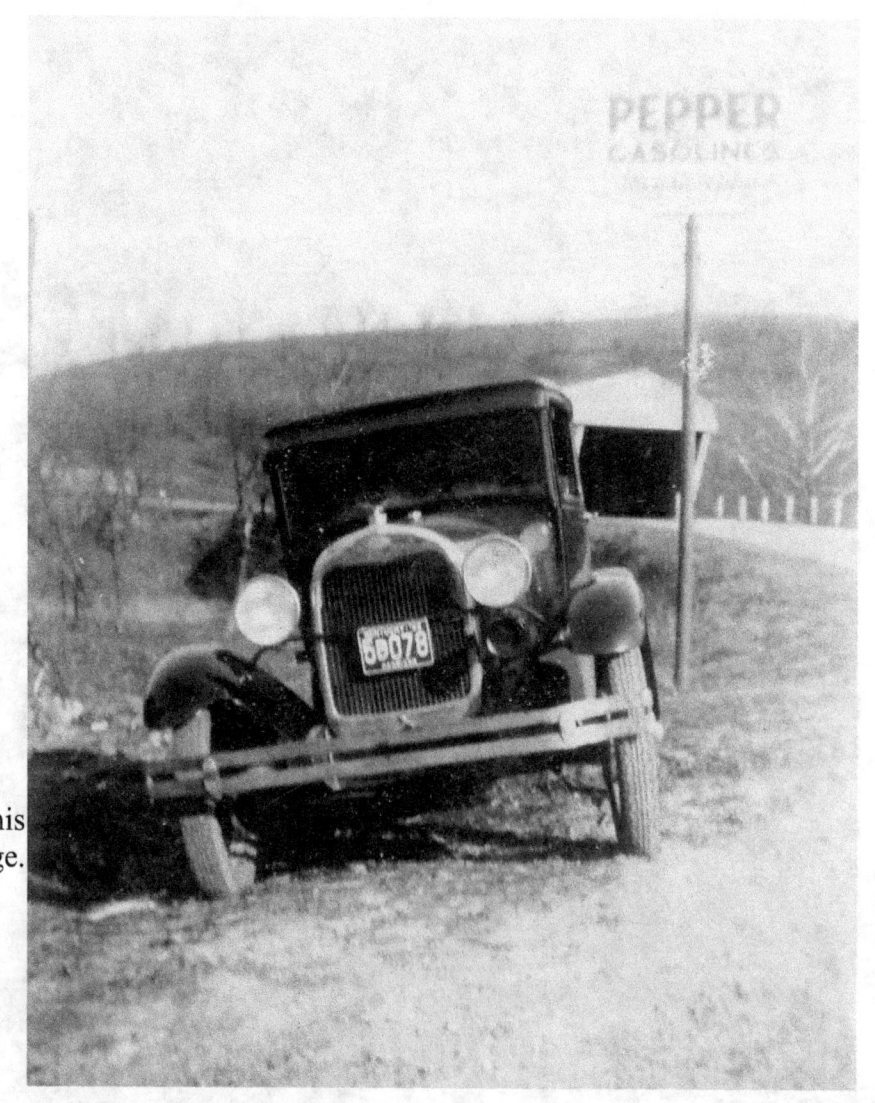

Bill Thompson and his
Ford Model A with the bridge.

1939

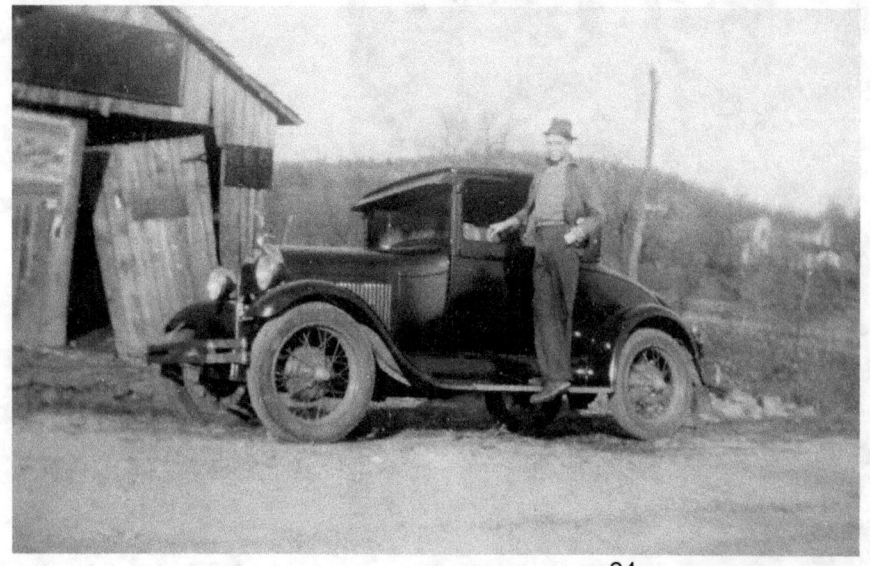

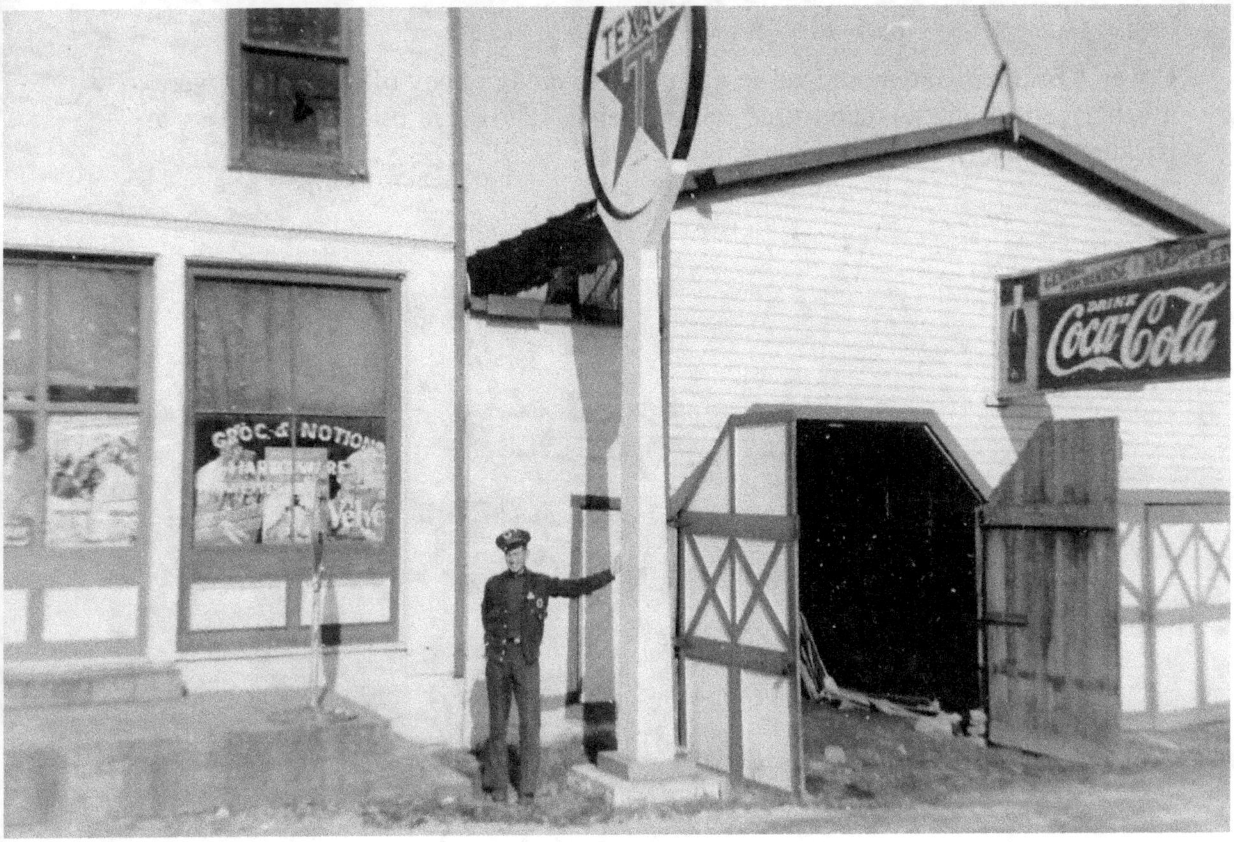

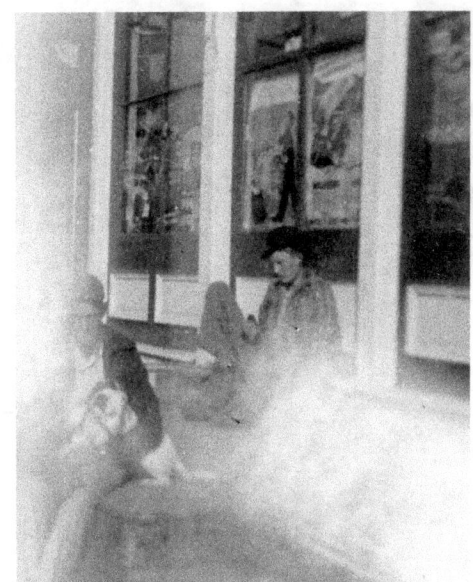

Bill Thompson in his Texaco uniform.

1940

Jim, Puffy and Paul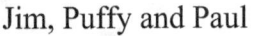

1939

Covered bridges were more than just a means to cross a body of water, they were much loved places to spend time with friends and were often included as a backdrop in many treasured photos.

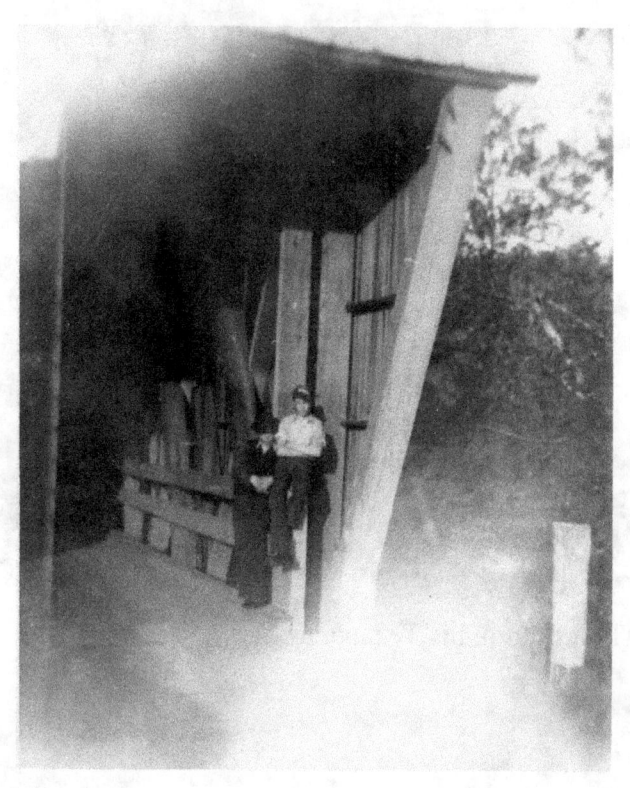

Charlie and Bill Thompson

1939

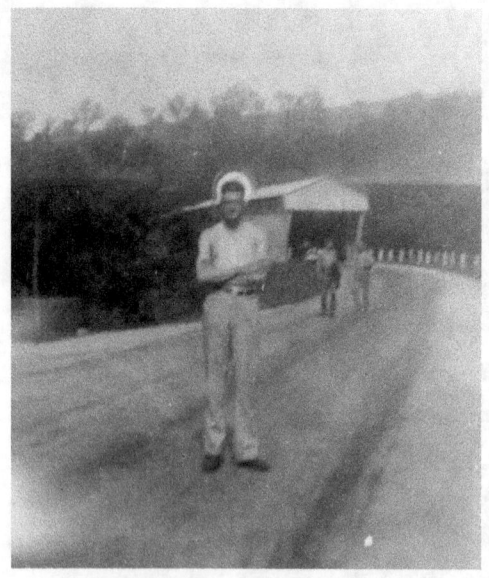

Beck

1938

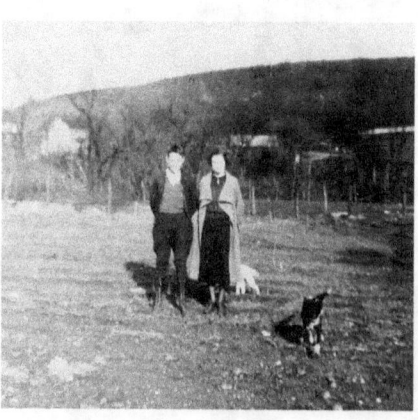

Jim Thompson and Eula Connor Watson

1936

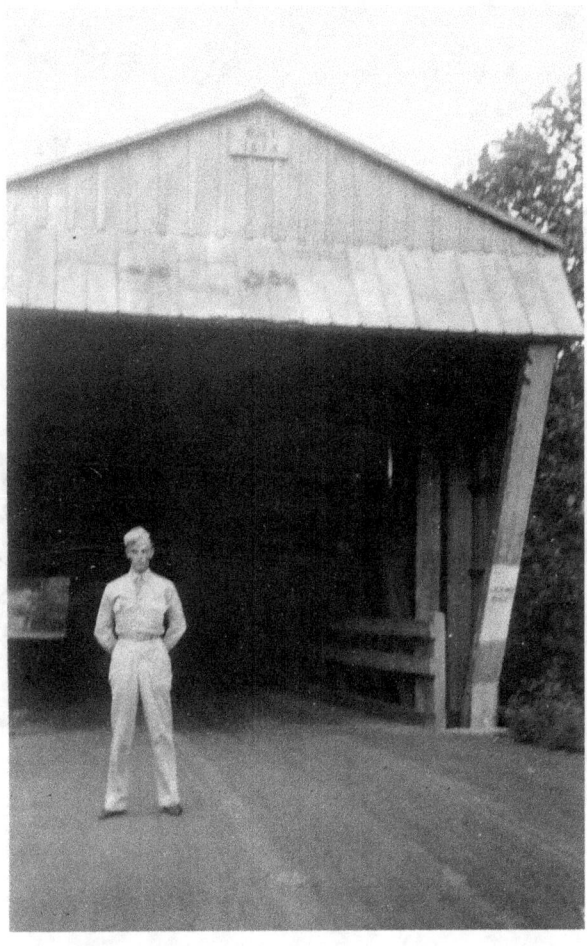

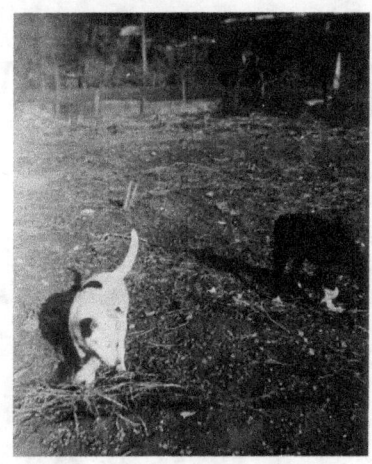

Puffy explores near the bridge with a friend.

1939

Billy Batte

1944

Claysville native and photographer, Eula Connor Watson documented her life in the hamlet with her camera. (The bridge is to her right.) Unfortunately none of her photos are known to exist today.

1936

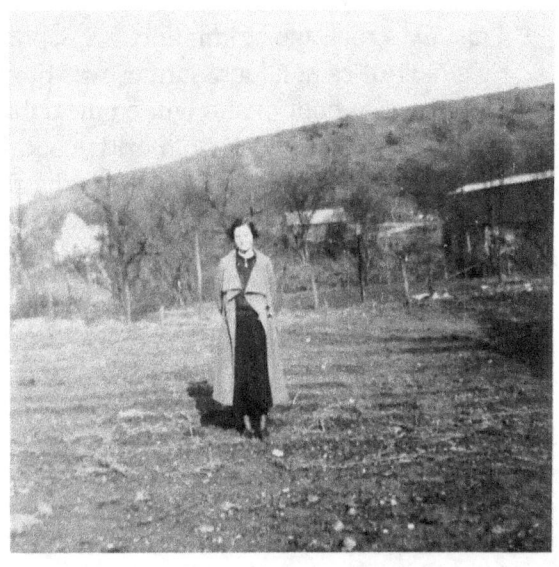

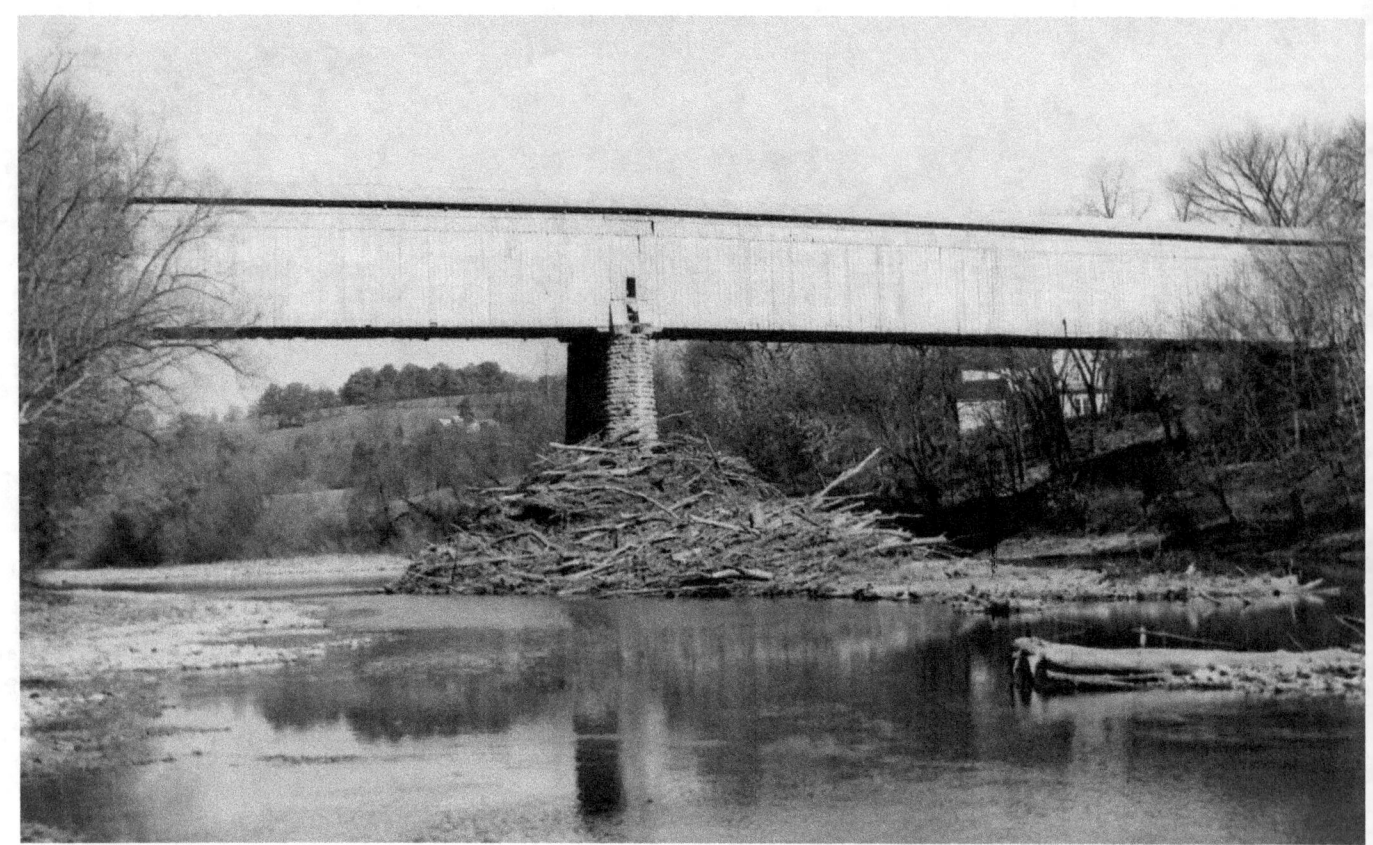

Tragedy struck the community on September 29, 1953 when, despite the dry conditions caused by a lack of rain, a local farmer was burning brush and trash on the riverbank. The fire quickly spread out of control and ignited the debris pile at the center pier of the bridge. Nothing could be done to save the 79 year old bridge and it collapsed into the river in a matter of minutes. There were reports of seeing smoke from the fire in Alexandria 40 miles away and the smell of smoke and creosote lingered in the Claysville area for days. The fire also burned a barn full of tobacco belonging to Herbert Batte, a corn field and nearly the general store.

Editor's note: The following account of the fire that destroyed the Claysville covered bridge is reprinted from the *Cynthiana Democrat* files.

Sept. 29, 1953, was a blistering hot day, with a dry wind blowing loose dust across Harrison County farmland.

There had been no rain for many days.

It was on that day that a man reportedly decided to burn some brush beneath the Claysville bridge.

His decision cost the community its wooden covered bridge that spanned the Main Licking River on U.S. 62 as well as a barn owned by Herbert Batte.

The brush fire ignited driftwood that in turn ignited the bridge. By 1 p.m., the Harrison County landmark was gone.

Batte, whose house sits near where the bridge stood, was working on his farm that day, and when he saw what was happening, began to try to save the Batte home and other buildings.

He knew, he said, there would be no saving the bridge.

"The bridge wasn't long falling in," he said, "because of the awfully dry timber."

"Fire was scattered every place — it surrounded us as it burned half way up the hill."

Charlie and Eula Watson were home that day, too. Mrs. Watson, who records life at Claysville with her camera, drove with her husband to the burning bridge, where she took several pictures of the burning structure.

At first residents were advised to travel either U.S. 68 or U.S. 27 to go from one side of the river to the other. But travelers also forded the river at Claysville at a place bulldozed by the Cynthiana Chamber of Commerce.

There wasn't a day, recalled Batte and the Watsons, when a car couldn't ford the river at Claysville, because the Licking remained so low that year.

But as tobacco selling season approached, farmers and warehousemen became concerned about the lack of a bridge at Claysville.

So a temporary Bailey bridge was put in place. The Watsons were there watching that, too. "They pushed it across one piece at a time with a bulldozer," said Watson. "It took them about 10 days to finish it."

According to an account of the fire in the Oct. 1, 1953, issue of the *Cynthiana Democrat* the Claysville bridge was the last covered bridge in the county, spanning 304 feet.

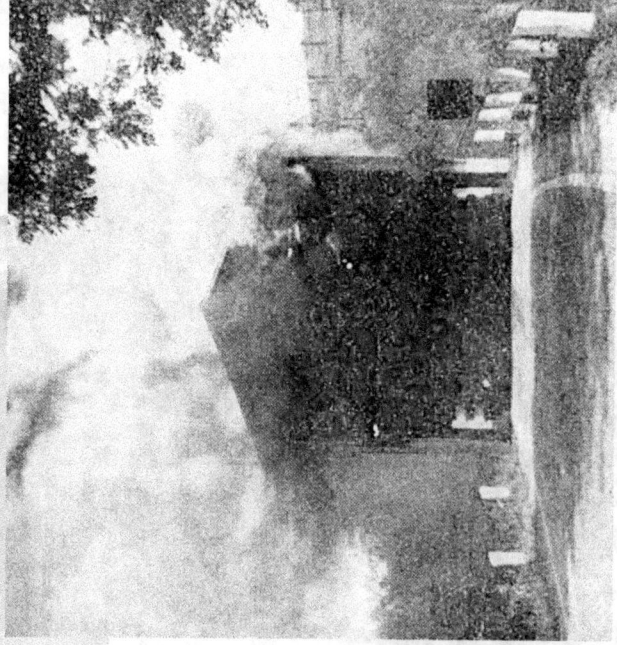

This article is from the July 1, 1993 special edition of the Cynthiana Democrat

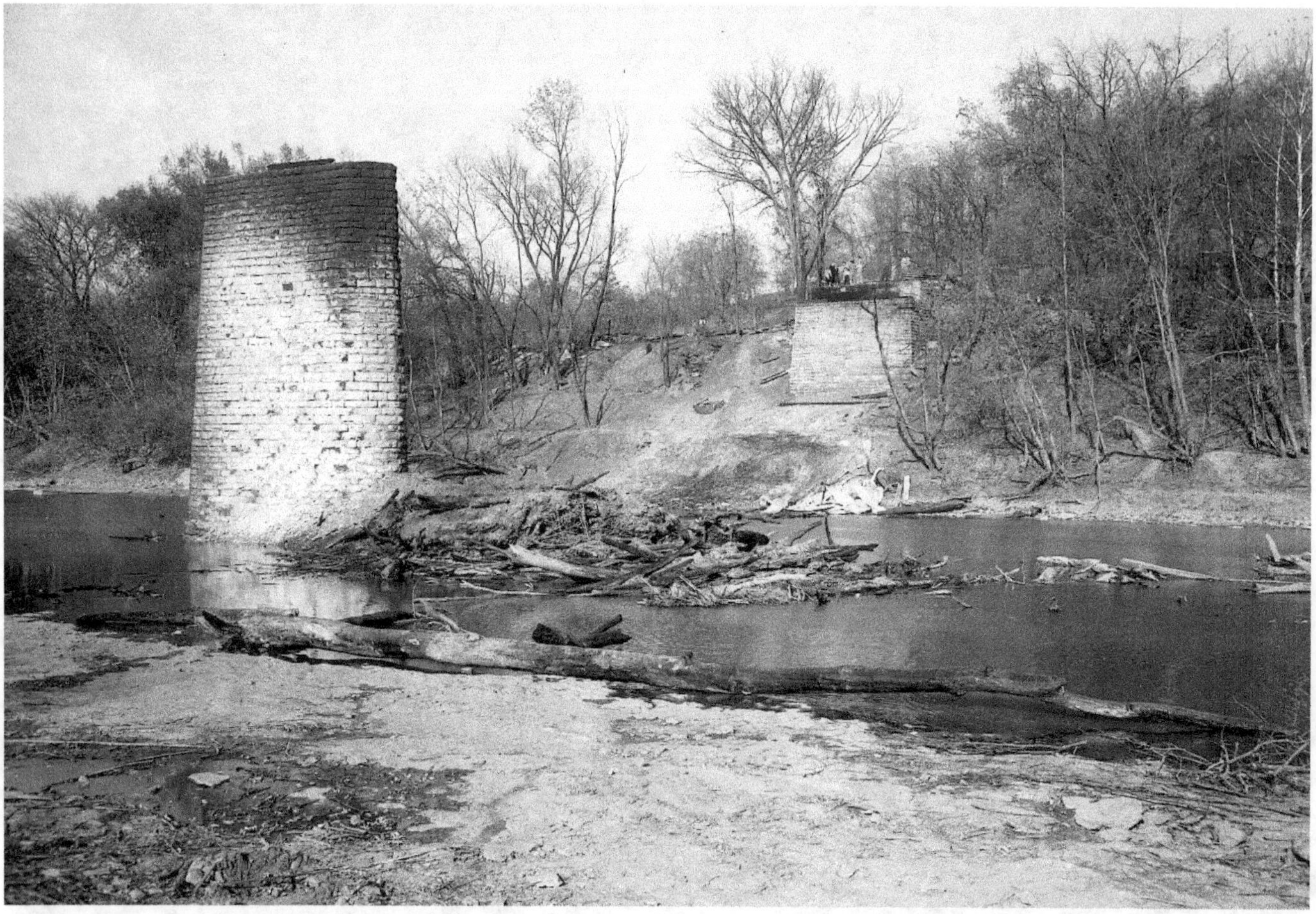

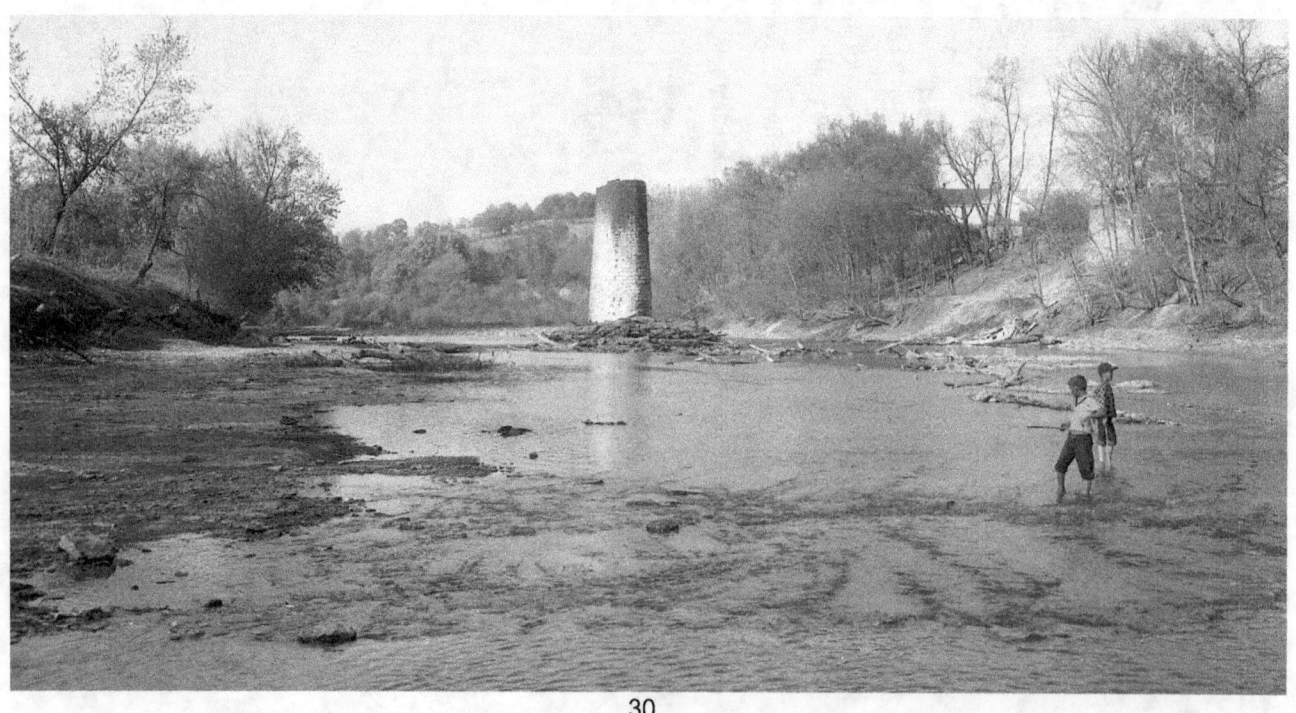

October 10, 1953

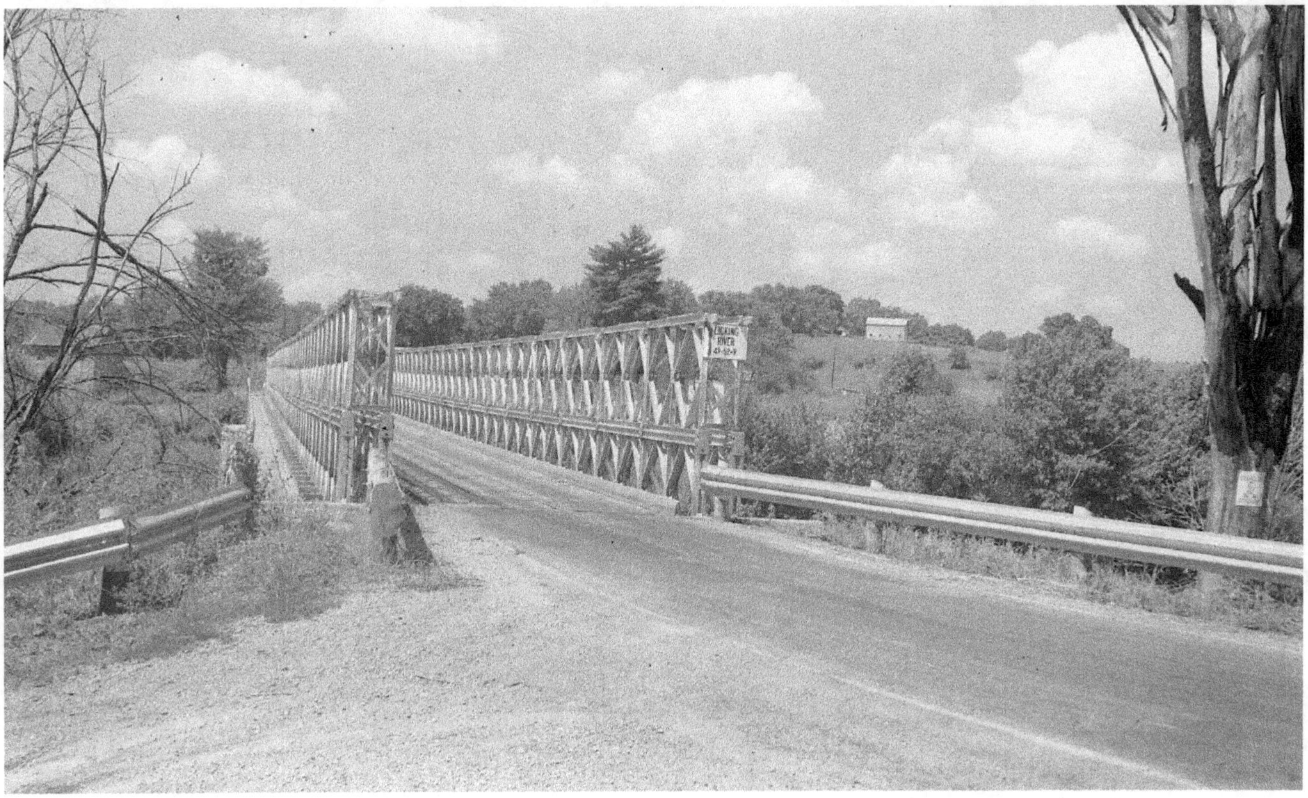

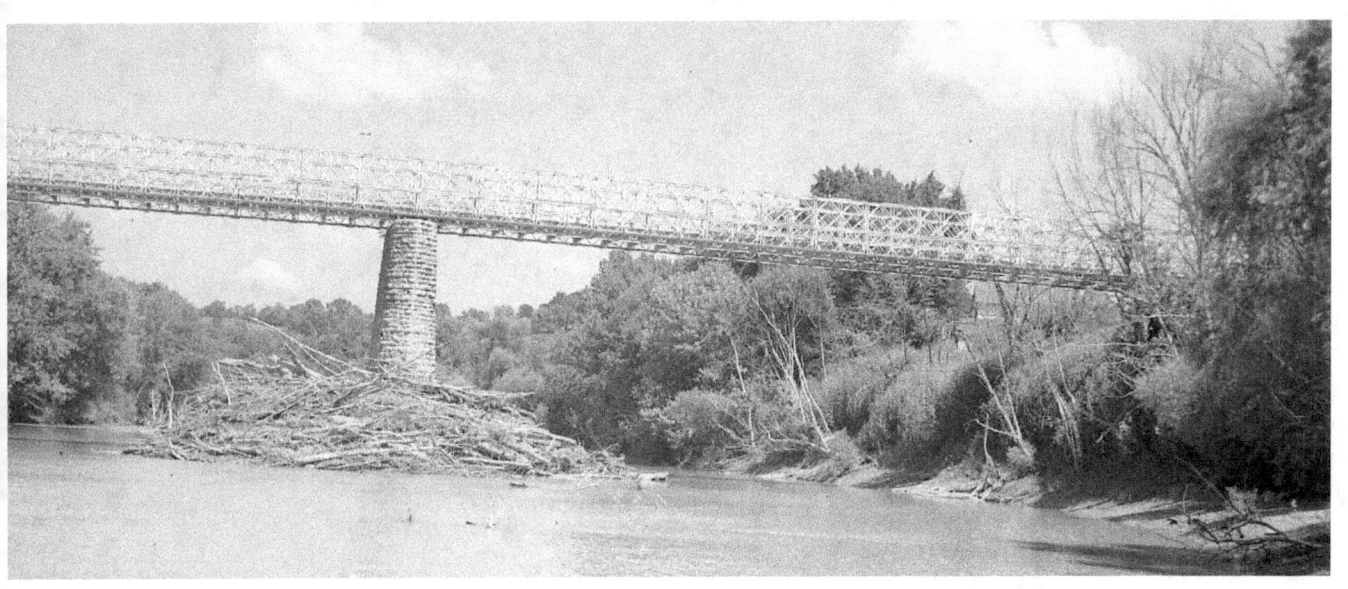

The temporary replacement Bailey Bridge lacked the aesthetics of the covered bridge. (Note the burned tree to the right of the bridge, another casualty of the fire.) Bailey Bridges were temporary, prefabricated truss bridges developed during WWII.

Cynthiana

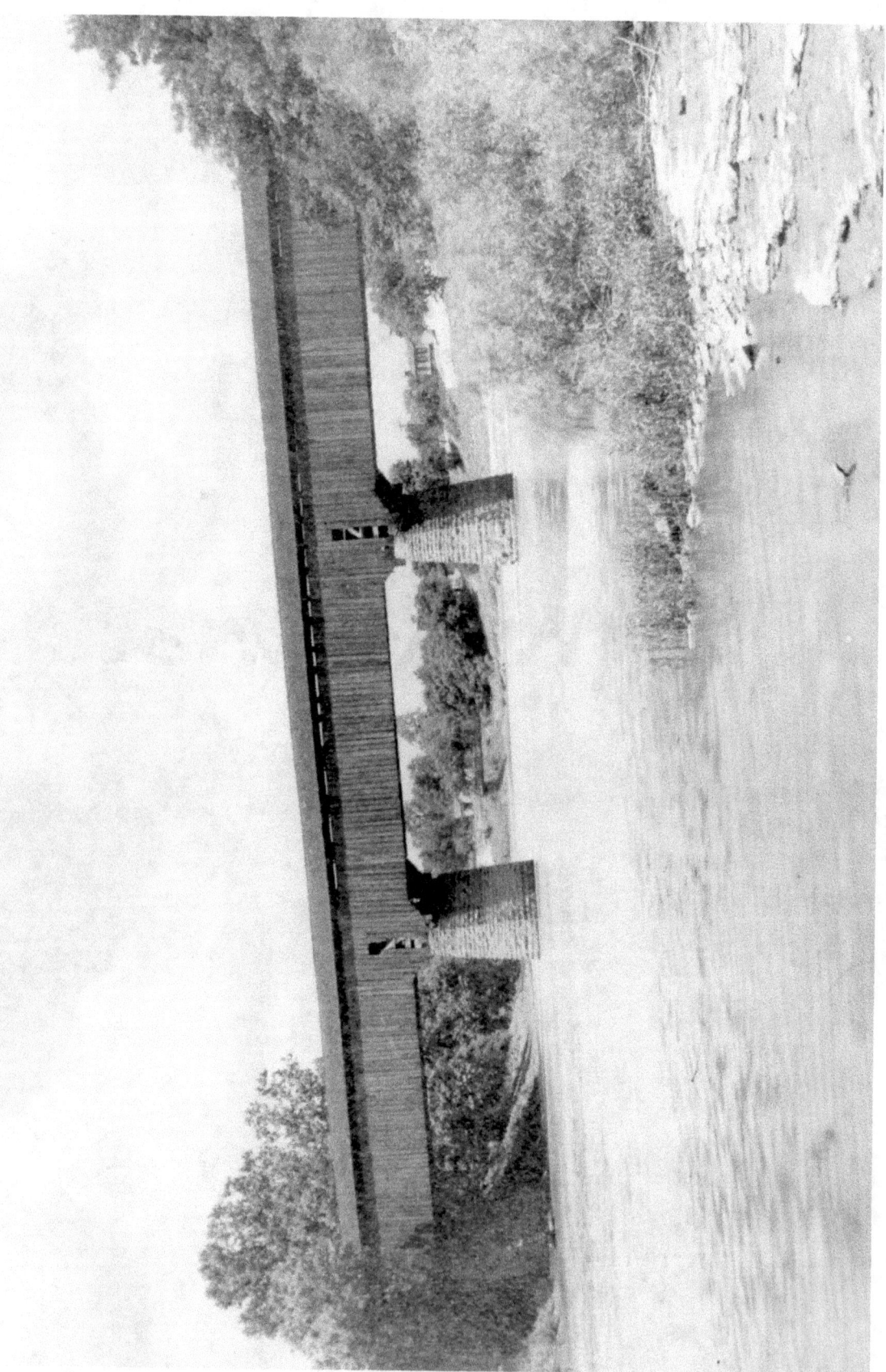

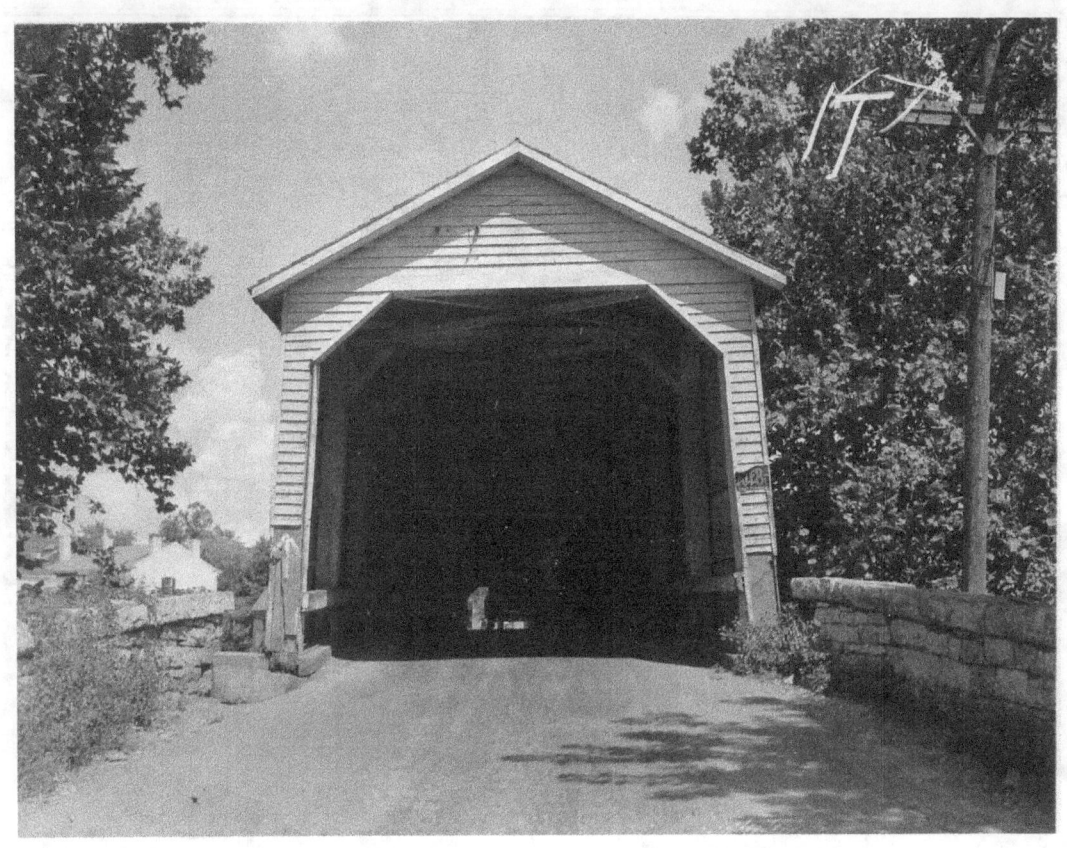

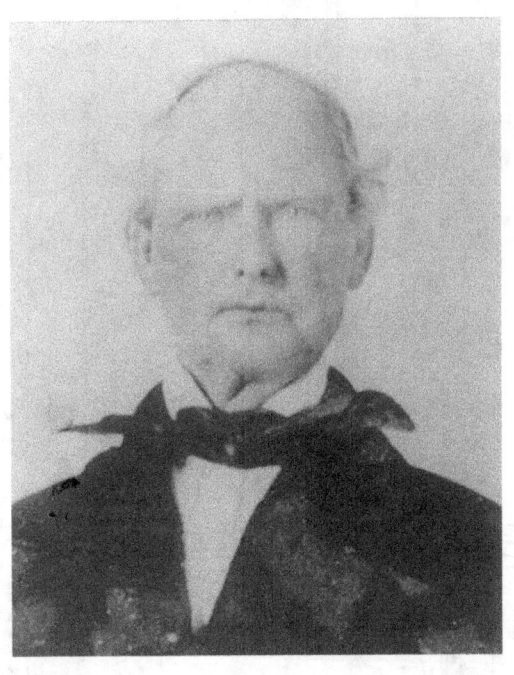

In 1837 Cynthiana resident and engineer Greenup Remington was contracted to construct what would become one of the state's most famous covered bridges across the South Fork of the Licking River at the entrance to Cynthiana. Plans for the bridge were reportedly drawn by master covered bridge builder, Lewis Wernwag.

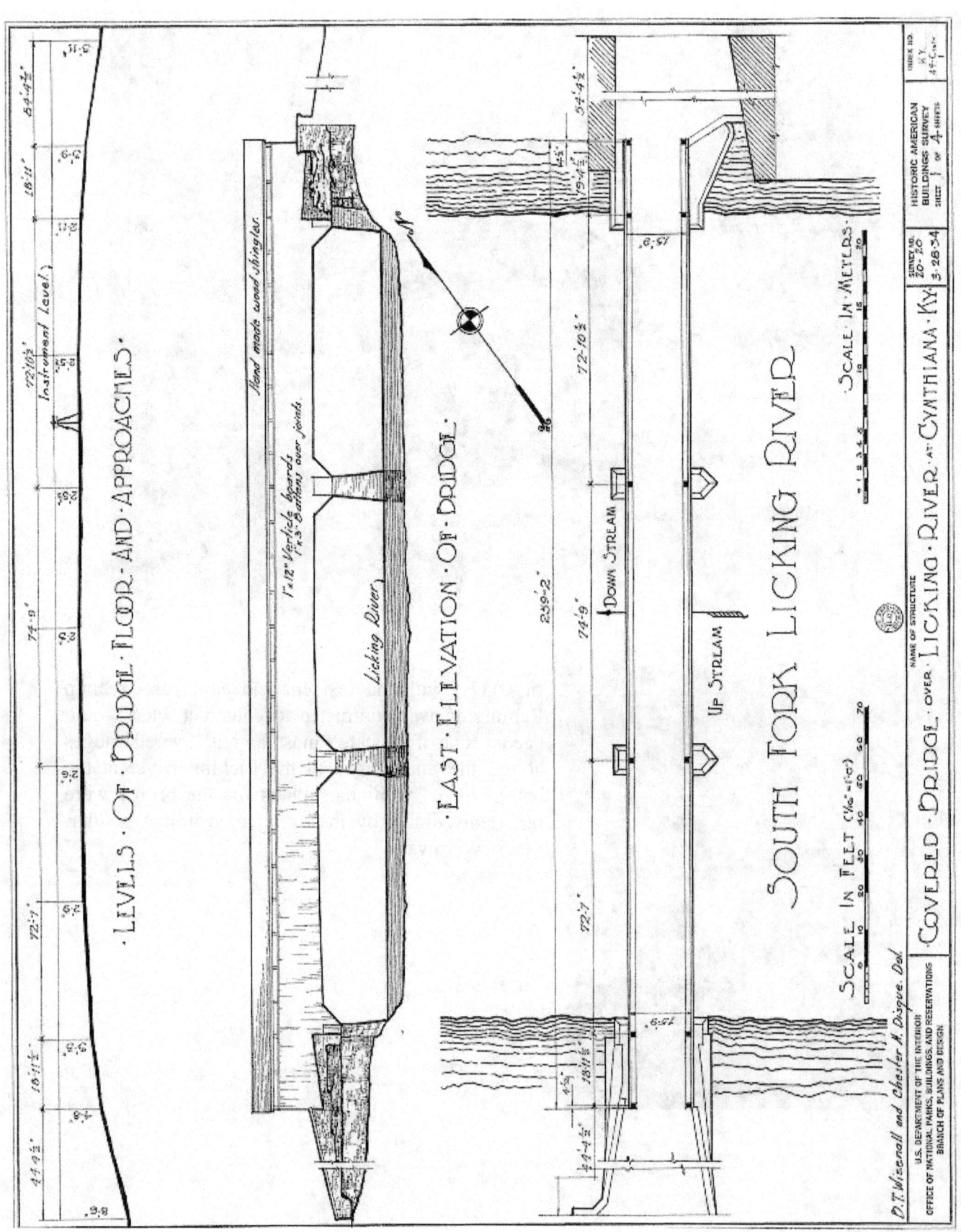

· LEVELS · OF · BRIDGE · FLOOR · AND · APPROACHES ·

· EAST · ELEVATION · OF · BRIDGE ·

SOUTH FORK LICKING RIVER

Licking River

Hand made wood shingles.

1"x12" Verticle boards
1"x3" Battens over joints.

DOWN STREAM

UP STREAM

SCALE IN FEET (3/16"=1'-0")

SCALE IN METERS

O.T. Wissenall and Chester N. Dague, Del.

U.S. DEPARTMENT OF THE INTERIOR
OFFICE OF NATIONAL PARKS, BUILDINGS, AND RESERVATIONS
BRANCH OF PLANS AND DESIGN

NAME OF STRUCTURE

COVERED · BRIDGE · OVER · LICKING · RIVER · AT · CYNTHIANA · KY.

SURVEY NO.
20-20
3-28-34

HISTORIC AMERICAN
BUILDINGS SURVEY
SHEET 1 OF 4 SHEETS

INDEX NO.
KY.
49-CYNTH
1

These 1935 drawings completed as part of the Historic American Buildings Survey conducted by the National Park Service give an idea of the complexity of the bridge's construction.

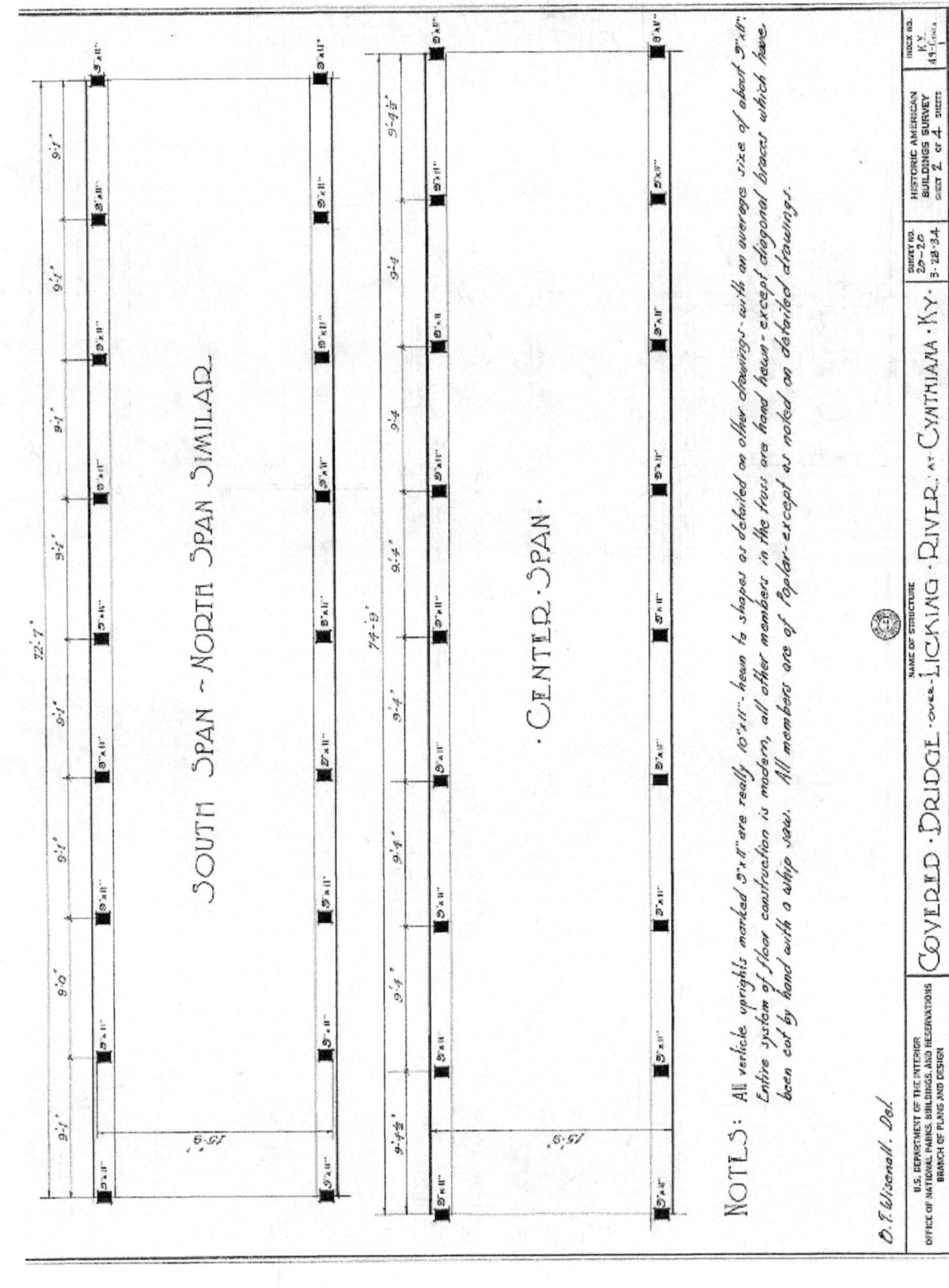

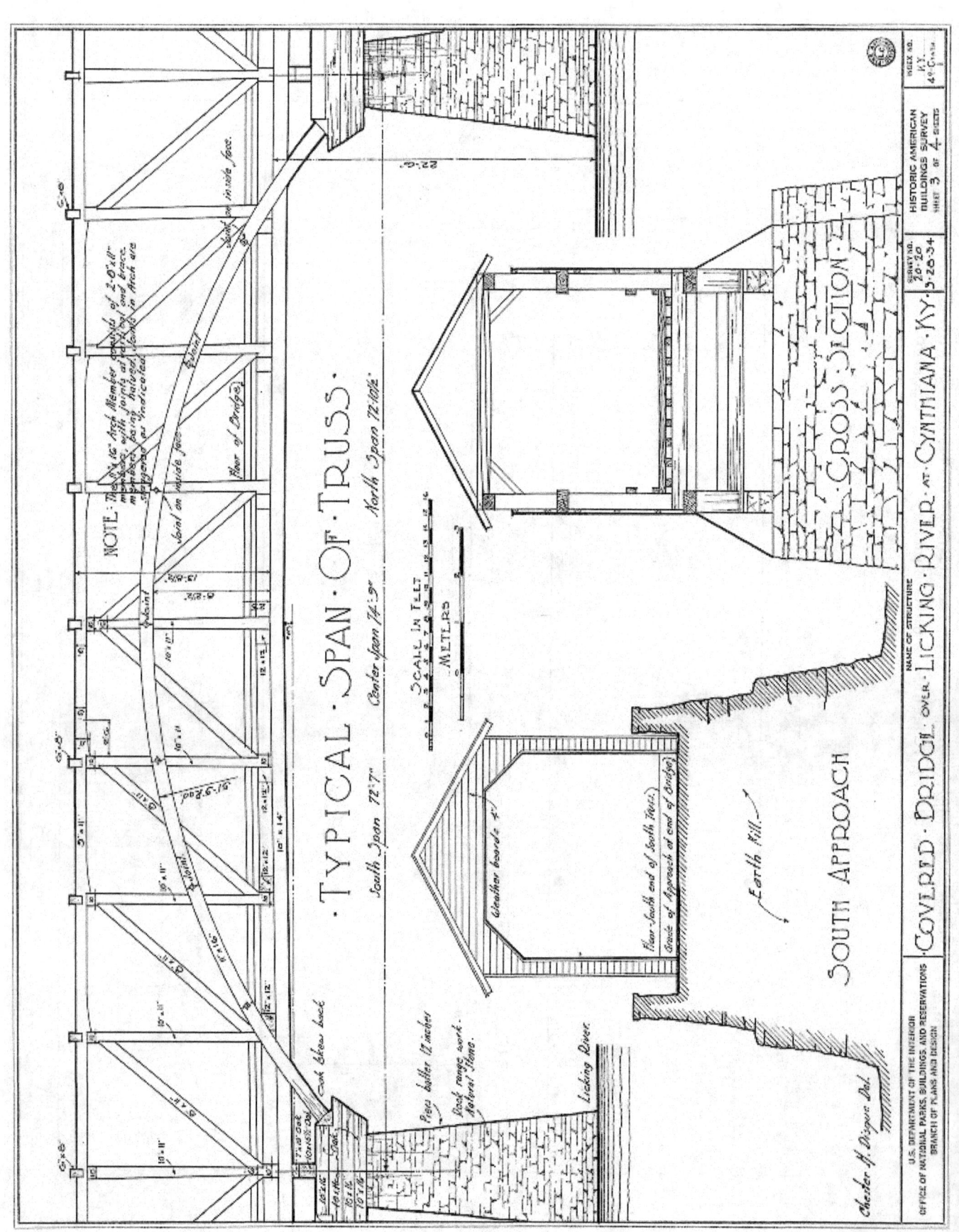

· TYPICAL · SPAN · OF · TRUSS ·

South Span 72'-7"   Center Span 74'-5"   North Span 72'-10½"

NOTE : The 2½ x 16" Arch Member consists of 2-2'-0 x 8" members bolted, with joints at each ¼ panel and brace members. Being tenoned, joints in Arch are staggered, as indicated.

SCALE IN FEET

METERS

CROSS SECTION

SOUTH APPROACH

COVERED · BRIDGE · over · LICKING · RIVER · at · CYNTHIANA · KY · 3-26-34

U.S. DEPARTMENT OF THE INTERIOR
OFFICE OF NATIONAL PARKS, BUILDINGS, AND RESERVATIONS
BRANCH OF PLANS AND DESIGN

NAME OF STRUCTURE

SURVEY NR.
20-39

INDEX NO.
KY.
40 CLASS

HISTORIC AMERICAN
BUILDINGS SURVEY
SHEET 3 OF 4 SHEETS

Chester H. Dripps Del.

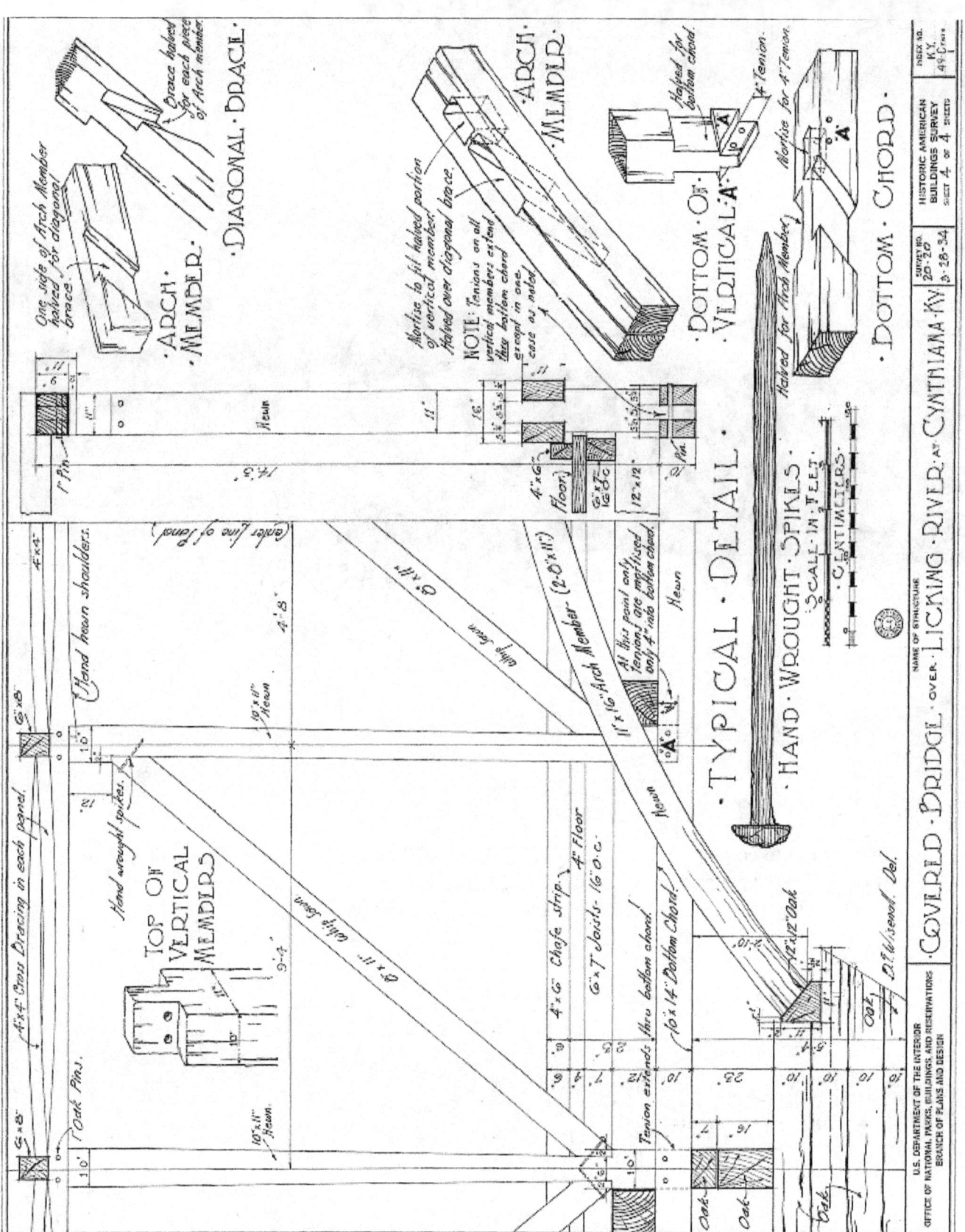

DIAGONAL·BRACE·

·ARCH·MEMBER·

·ARCH·MEMBER·

·BOTTOM·OF·VERTICAL·A·

·BOTTOM·CHORD·

·TYPICAL·DETAIL·

·HAND·WROUGHT·SPIKES·

·Scale·in·Feet·

·Centimeters·

·COVERED·BRIDGE·over·LICKING·RIVER·at·CYNTHIANA·KY.·

·TOP·OF·VERTICAL·MEMBERS·

U.S. DEPARTMENT OF THE INTERIOR
OFFICE OF NATIONAL PARKS, BUILDINGS, AND RESERVATIONS
BRANCH OF PLANS AND DESIGN

NAME OF STRUCTURE

SURVEY NO.
20·20

3·28·34

HISTORIC AMERICAN
BUILDINGS SURVEY
SHEET 4 OF 4 SHEETS

INDEX NO.
KY.
49·Cm·

D.W.Lenoir. Del.

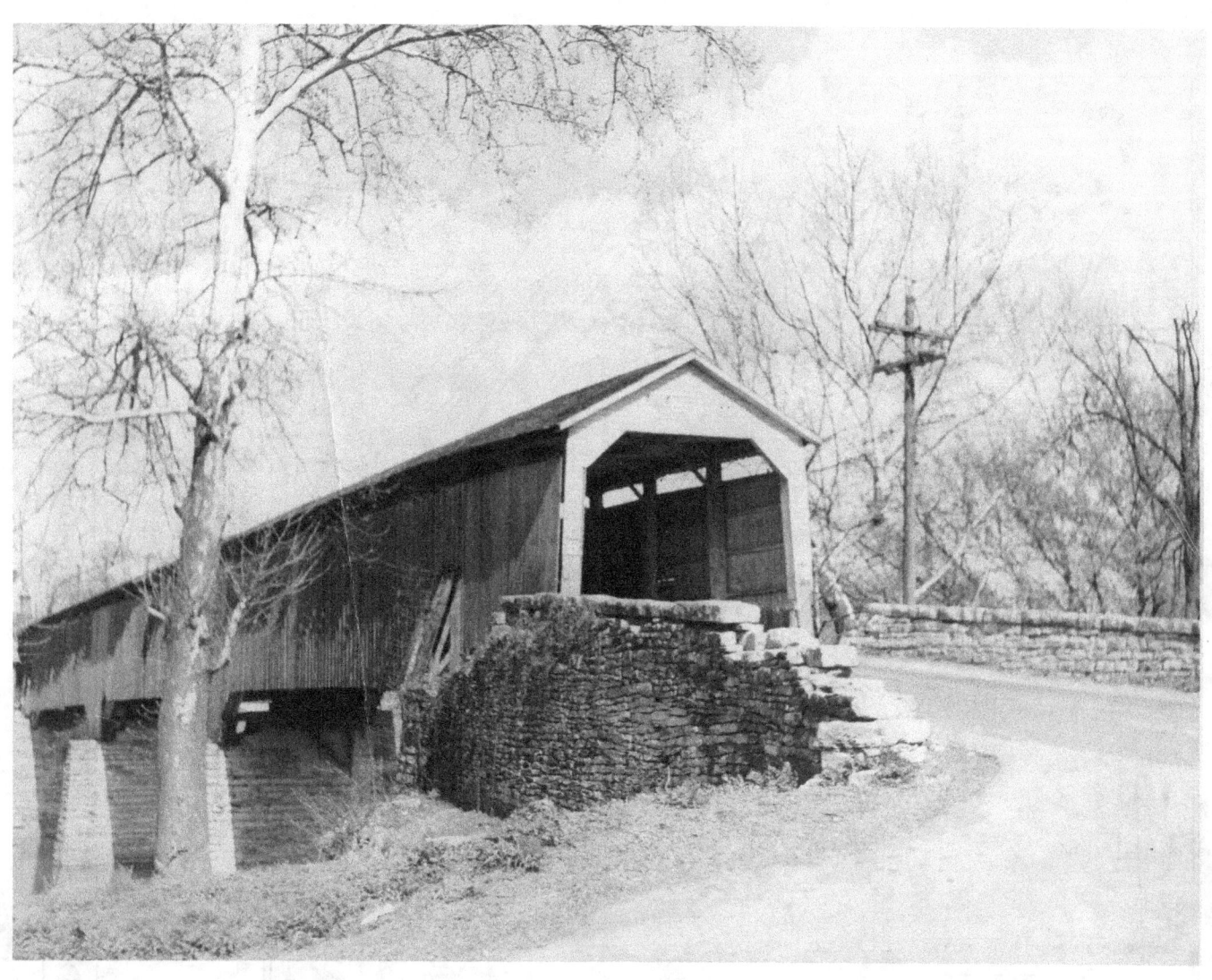

According to county records, the 1837 bridge was the third covered bridge built on the site, the first of which was built in 1807. The second was built in 1817, lasting only twenty years. No pictures have ever been discovered of the first two bridges.

If the bridge could talk, it would certainly have a tale to tell. It was a silent witness to the horrors and heartaches that were the Civil War. On July 17, 1862 General John Hunt Morgan's troops marched on Cynthiana. Rather than burning the bridge to prevent Morgan's troops from entering Cynthiana, Union General John J. Landrum preferred exchanging fire across the river and through the bridge. Finally the Confederate troops overpowered the Union Army, entered the city through the bridge and General Landrum's troops were forced to surrender.

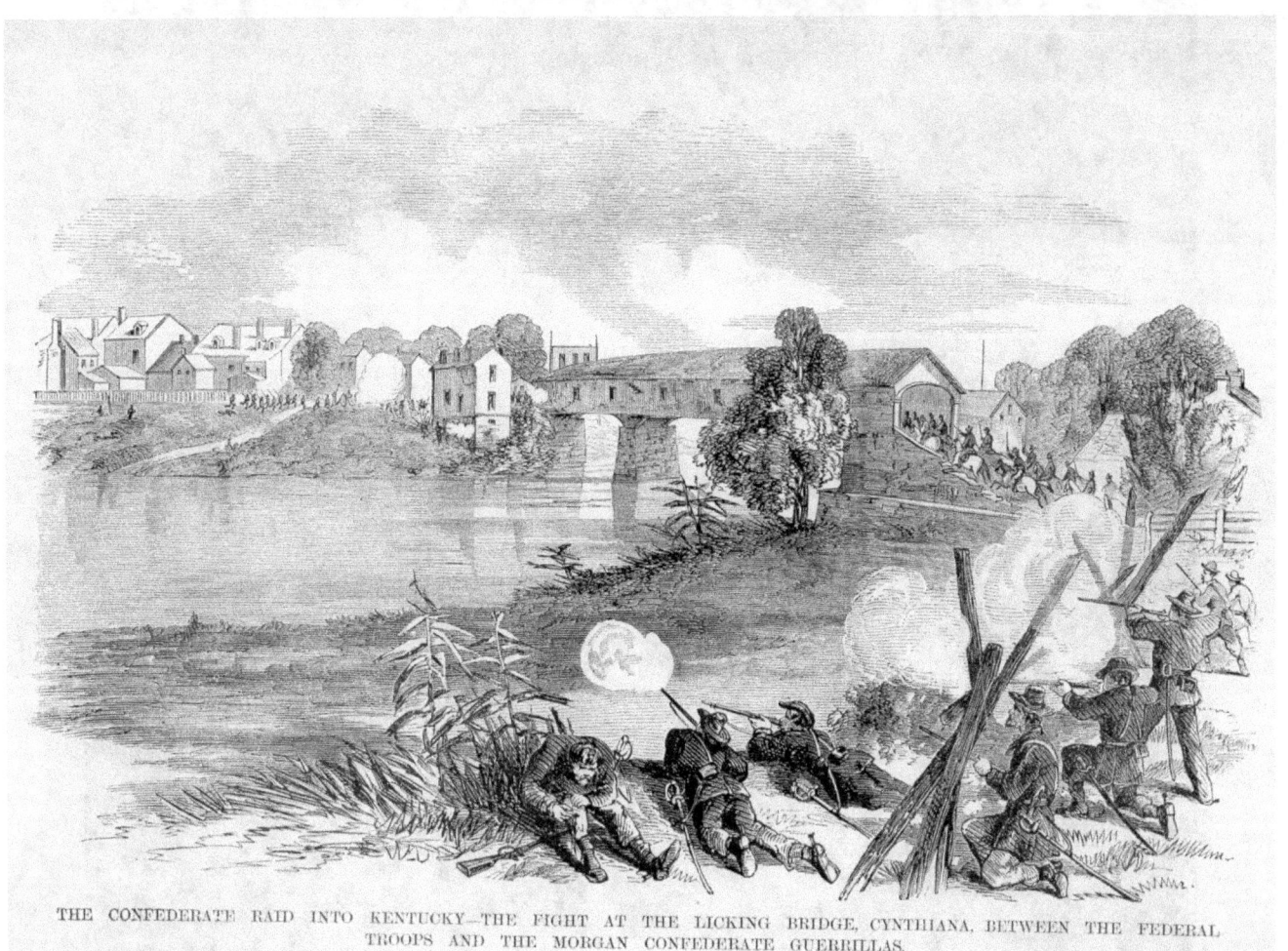

THE CONFEDERATE RAID INTO KENTUCKY—THE FIGHT AT THE LICKING BRIDGE, CYNTHIANA, BETWEEN THE FEDERAL TROOPS AND THE MORGAN CONFEDERATE GUERRILLAS.

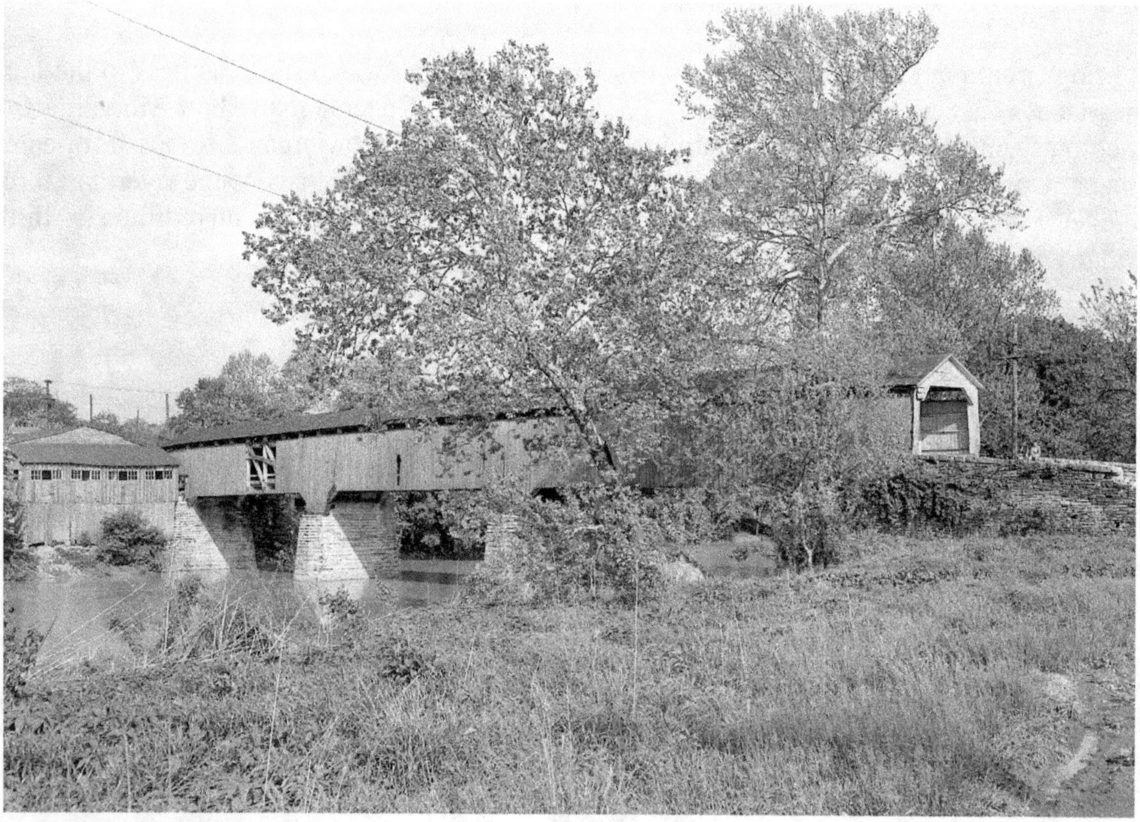

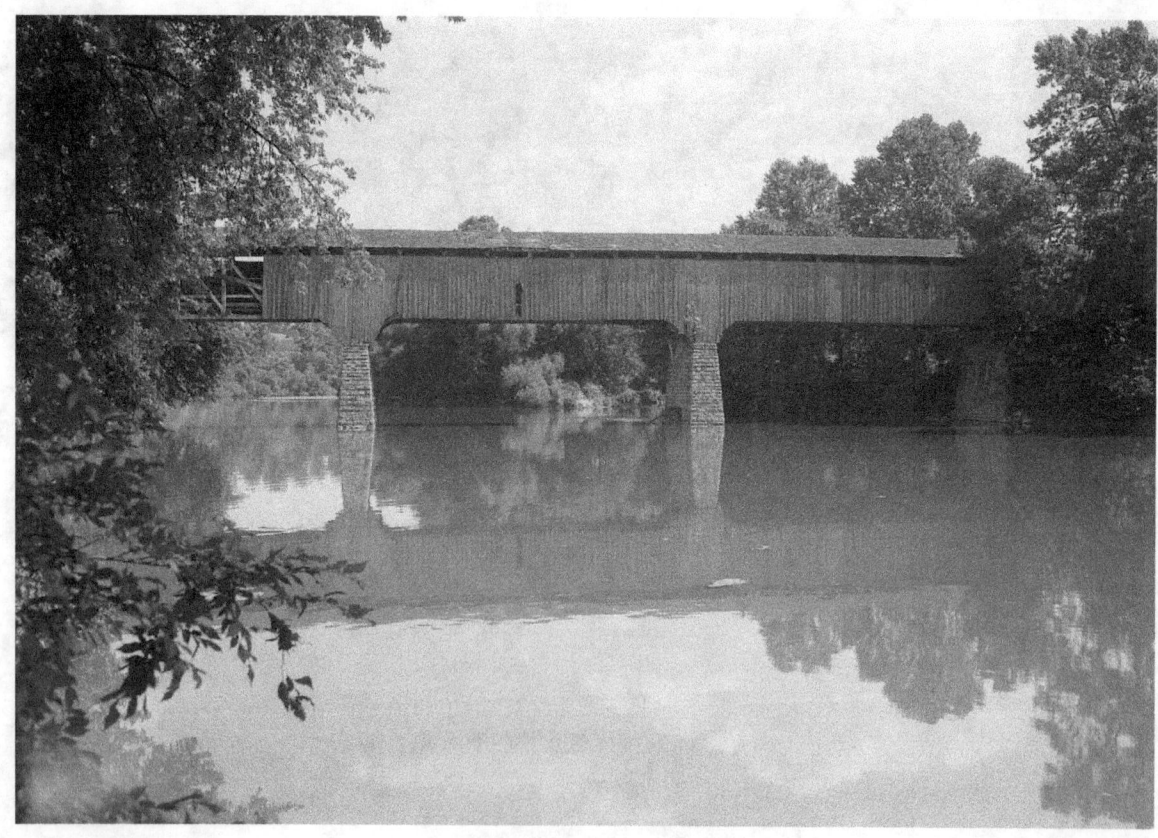

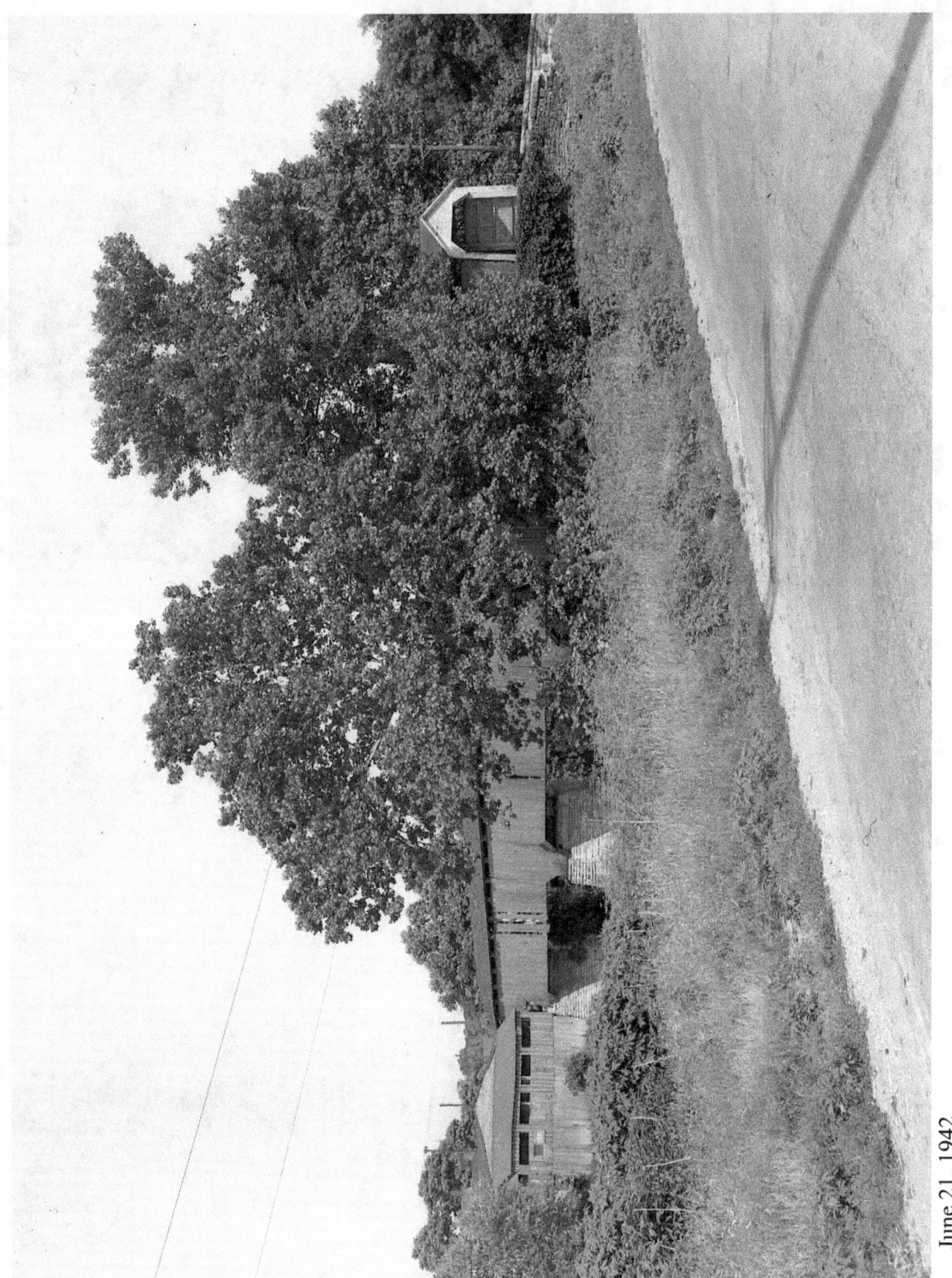

June 21, 1942

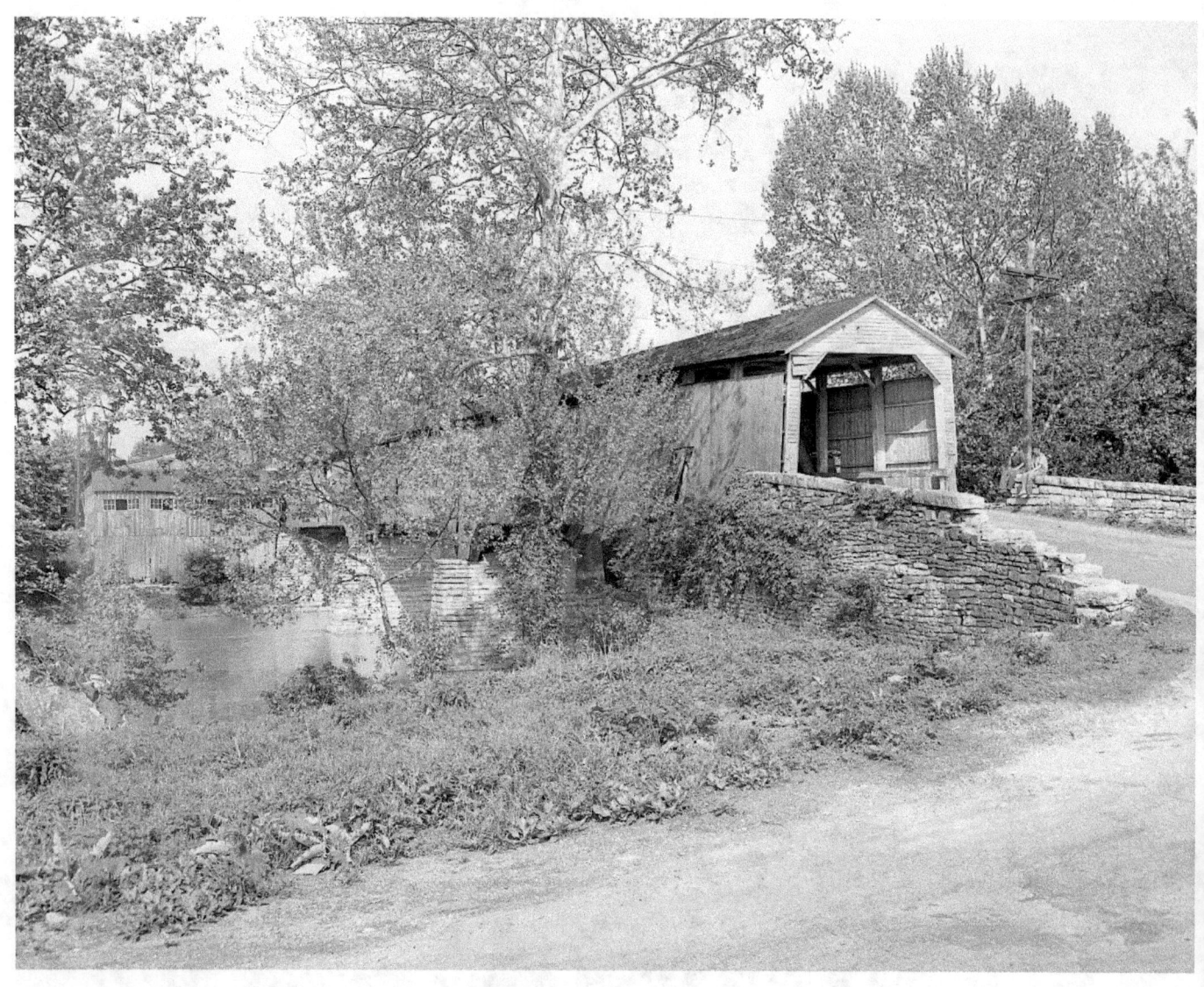

May 16, 1943

The bridge consisted of three spans and was 220 feet long.

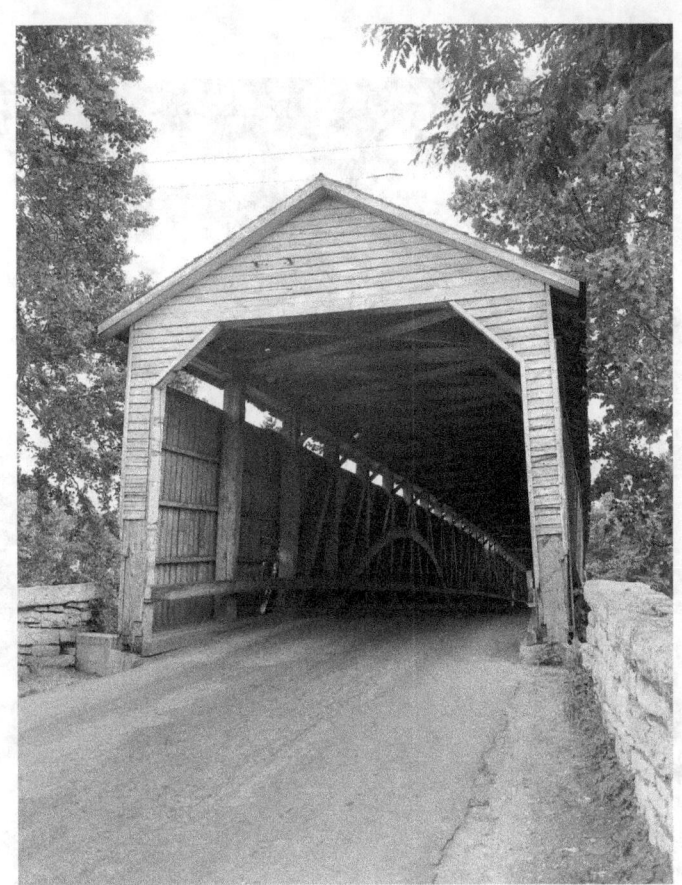

Taken from an unknown and undated newspaper article:

Spanning not only the river but also the chronological gap between the ox-cart and the streamlined automobile, the old bridge could tell a fascinating story of the traffic it has carried - of county fair and circus crowds, of travelers sheltered beneath its friendly roof and sudden showers, of clattering riders coming and going from County Court. It could tell of South Licking in flood, of lovers' trysts by moonlight, of the Harrison County boys who volunteered for the Mexican War. It could tell of days the 1860s, when Morgan and his swift riders dashed through it to capture Cynthiana from the Federals in 1862; of 1864 too, where the fortunes of war were reversed and some of these same riders galloping through it to escape capture; of 1898, when the boys entrained for Lexington and the Spanish-American War, and of 1917, when units marched away to World War I Camps.

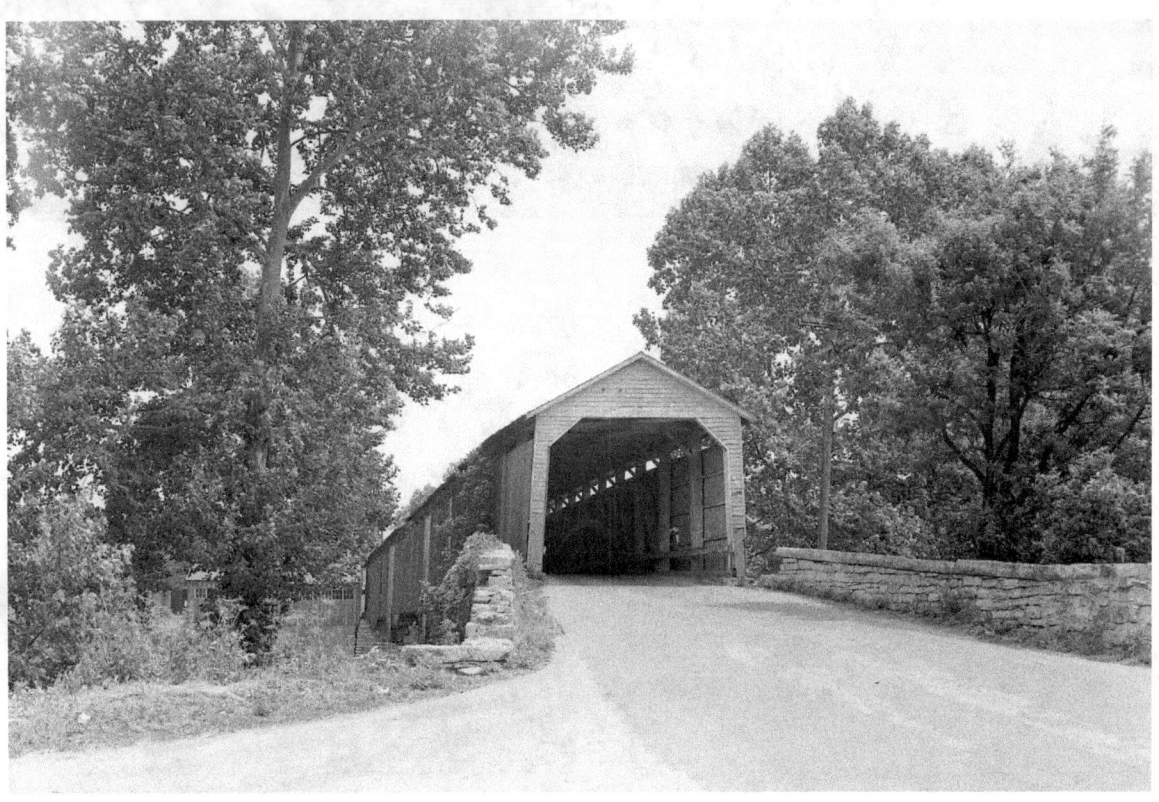

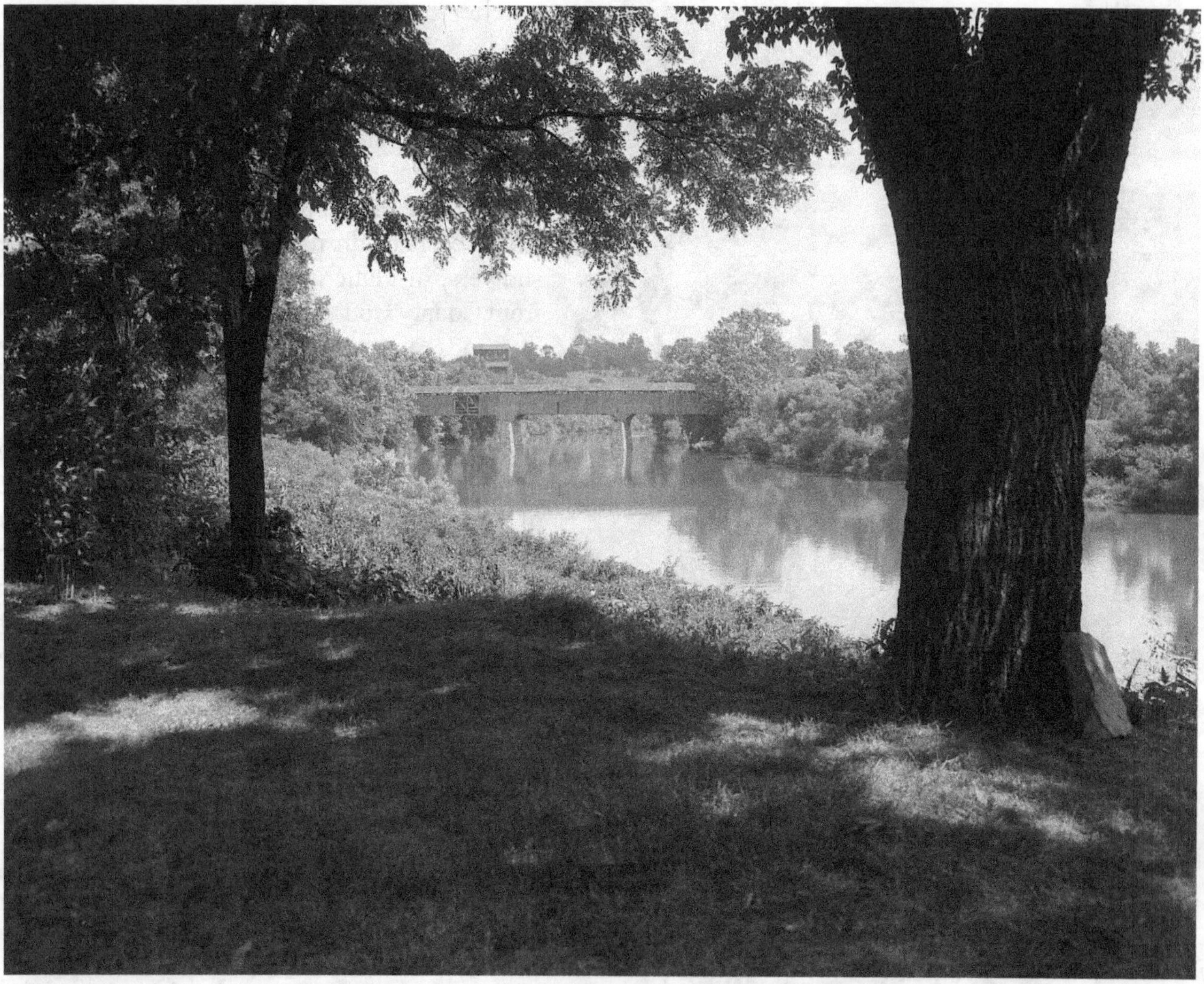

June 25, 1944

One can just imagine the youths of the county escaping the sun underneath these shade trees, fishing, roughhousing and watching the sparkling waters of the South Fork of the Licking lazily drift by.

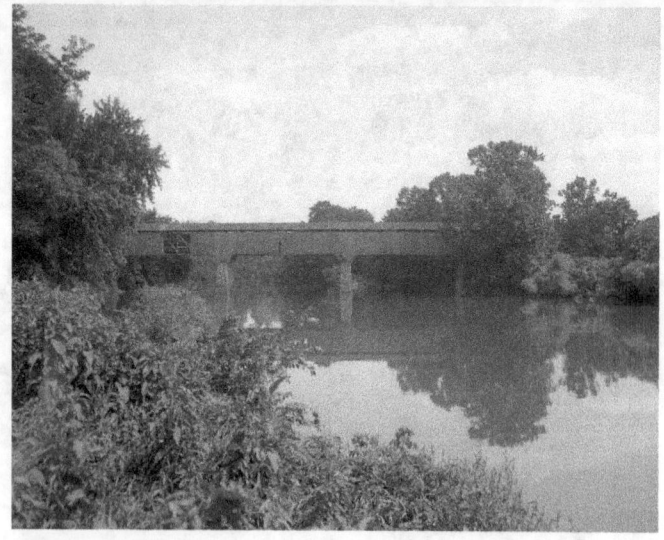

March 29, 1934

Cynthiana's bridge was often featured on postcards:

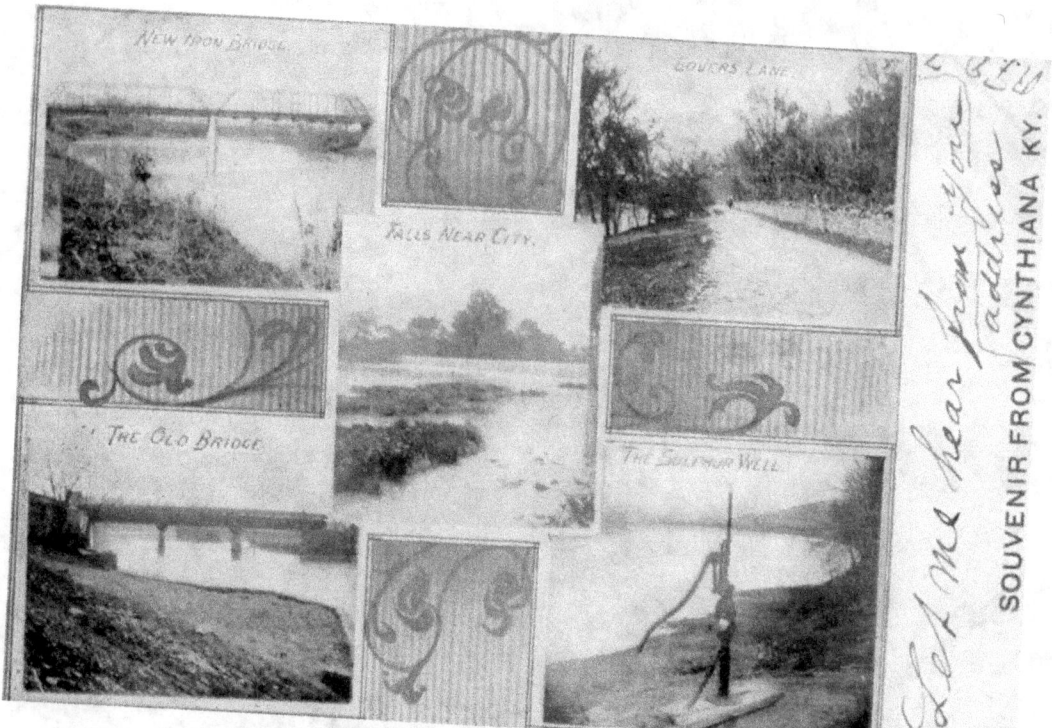

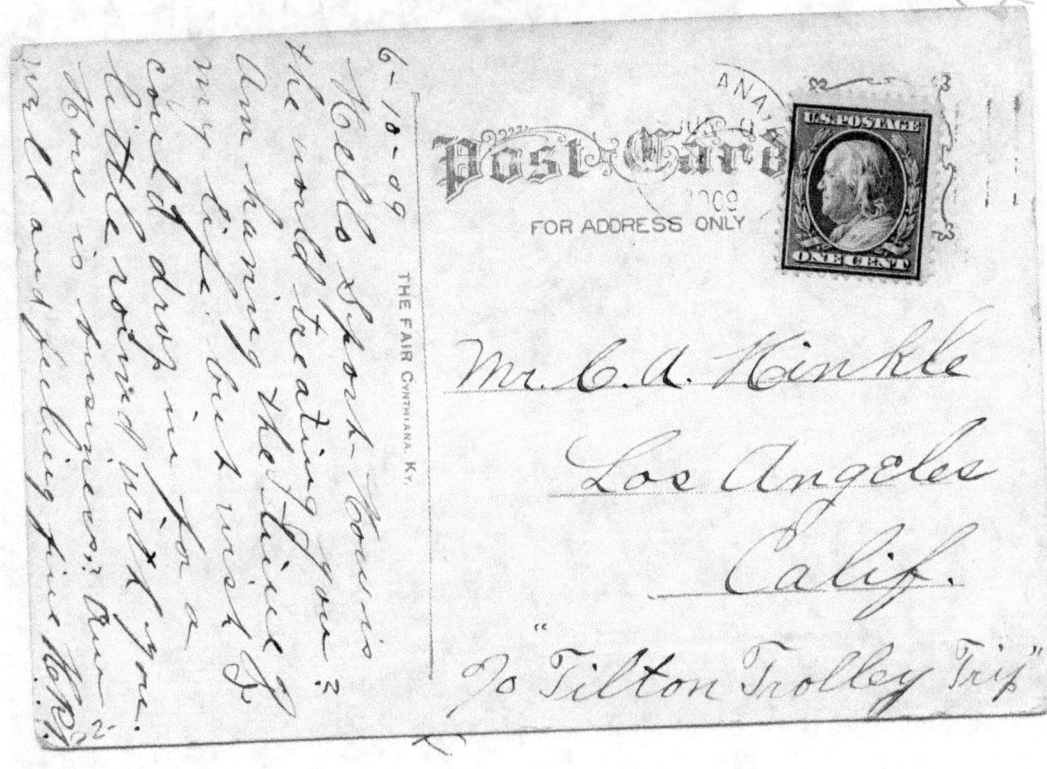

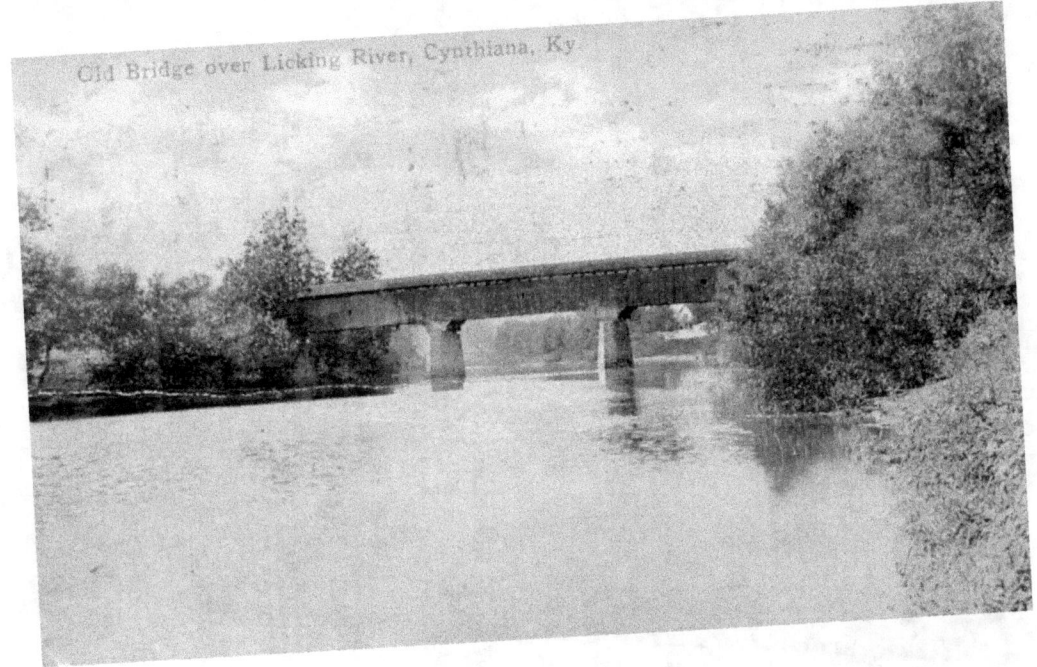

Old Bridge over Licking River, Cynthiana, Ky.

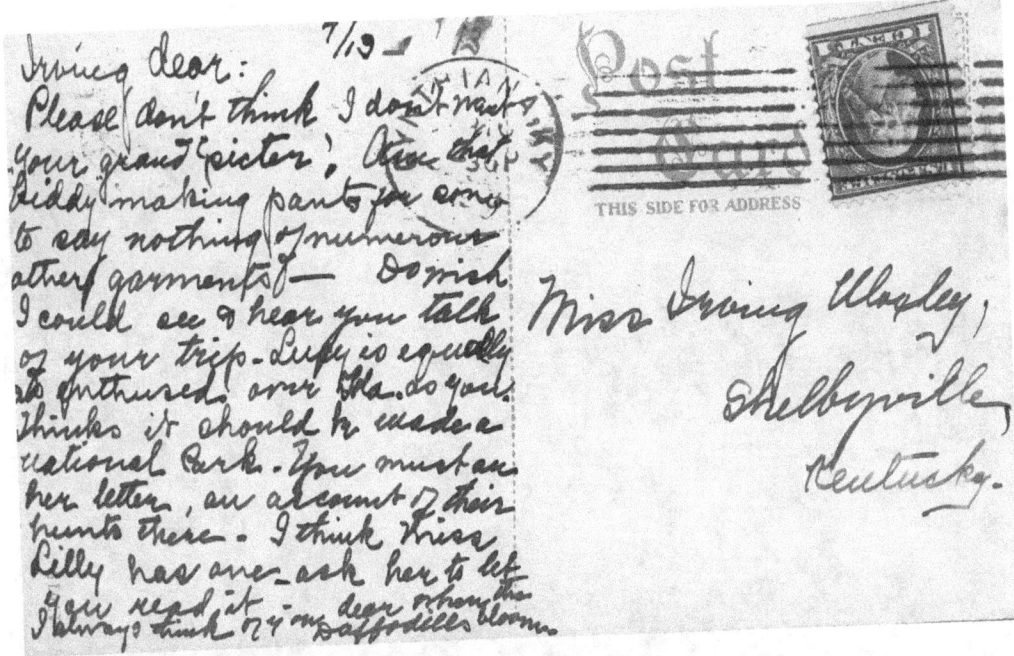

Irving dear:

Please don't think I don't want your grand "picter". Also that biddy making pants for one to say nothing of numerous other garments — Do wish I could see & hear you talk of your trip. Lucy is equally so enthused over Fla. do you thinks it should be made a national Park. You must ask her letter, an account of their hunts there — I think Miss Lilly has one — ask her to let you read it. —

I always think of you, dear, when the Daffodils bloom.

Post
Card

THIS SIDE FOR ADDRESS

Miss Irving Wooley,
Shelbyville,
Kentucky.

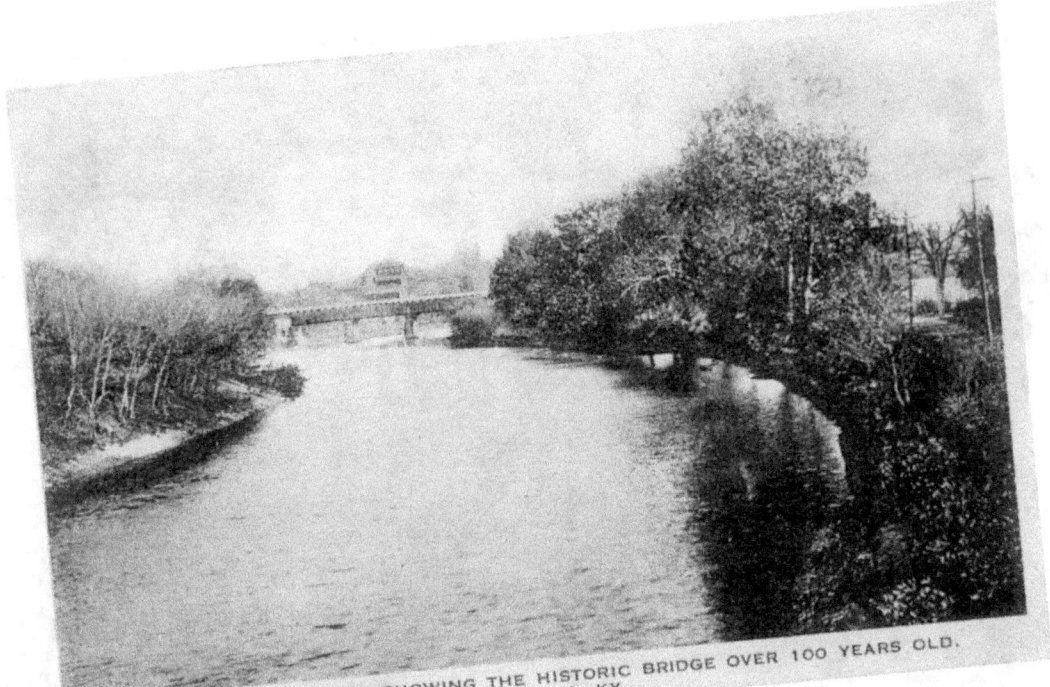

PICTURESQUE LICKING, SHOWING THE HISTORIC BRIDGE OVER 100 YEARS OLD.
CYNTHIANA, KY.

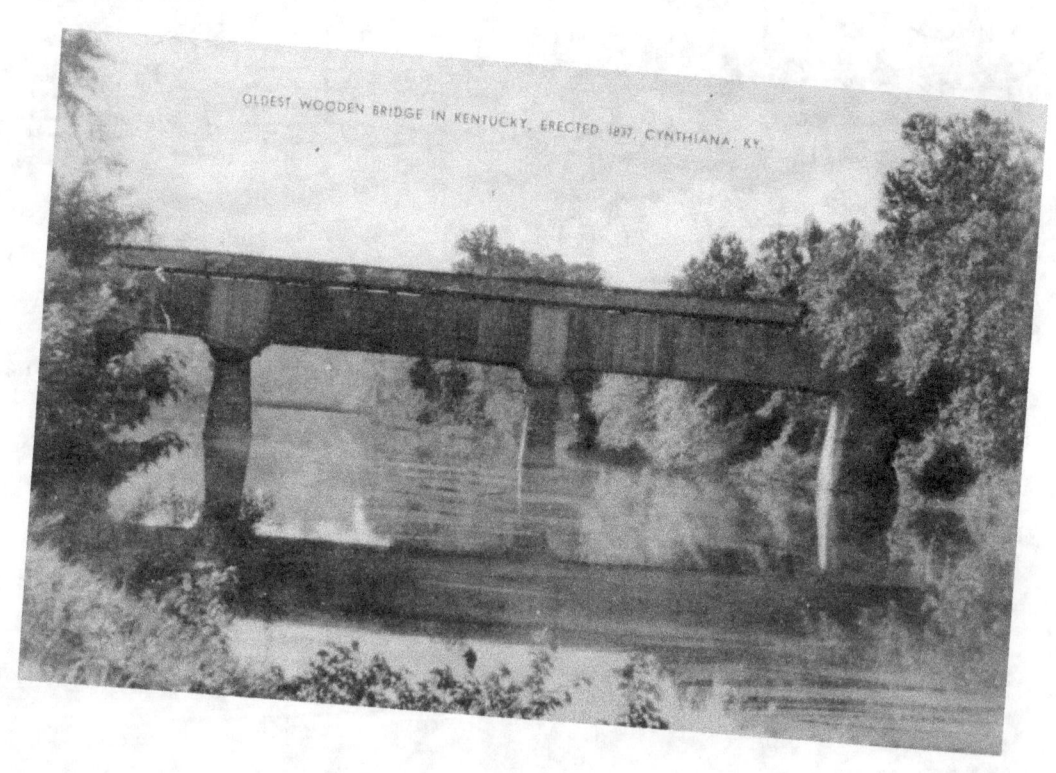

OLDEST WOODEN BRIDGE IN KENTUCKY, ERECTED 1837, CYNTHIANA, KY.

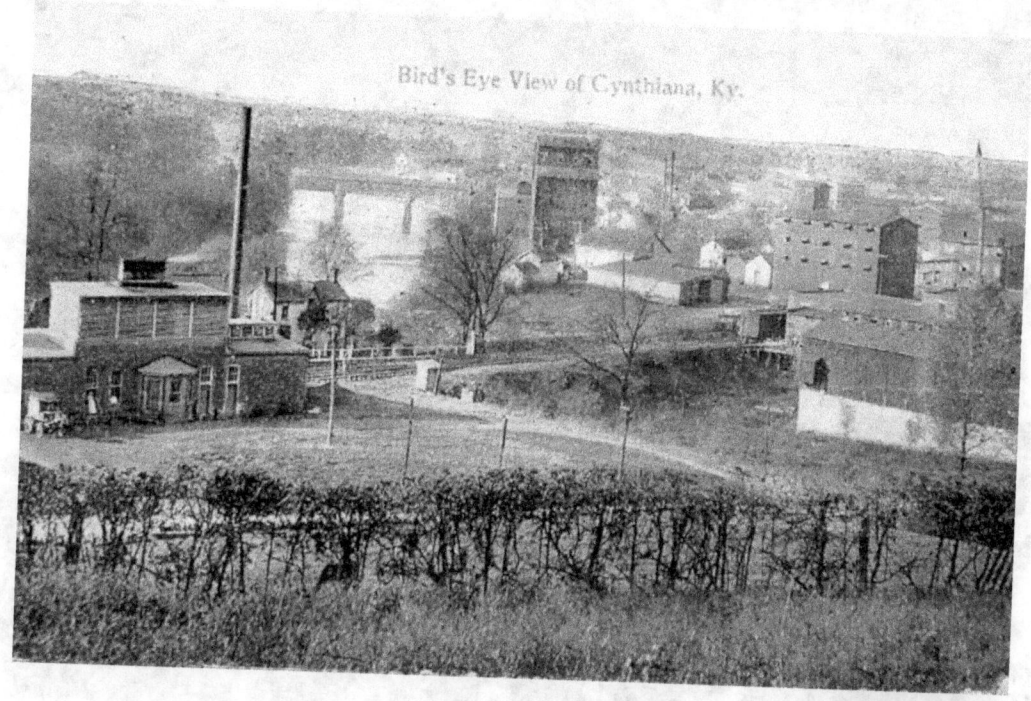

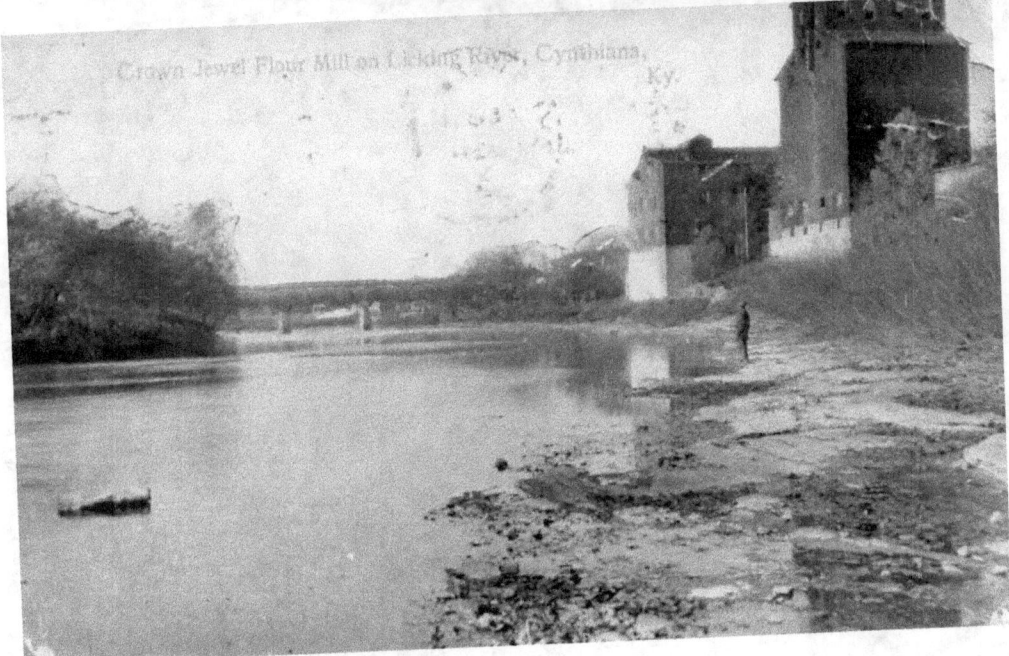

On these postcards you can see the Crown Jewel Flour Mill with the bridge in the background. Erected in 1809 the buildings first housed a woolen factory, then a cotton mill and various other businesses until the Crown Jewel Milling Company was incorporated in 1905.

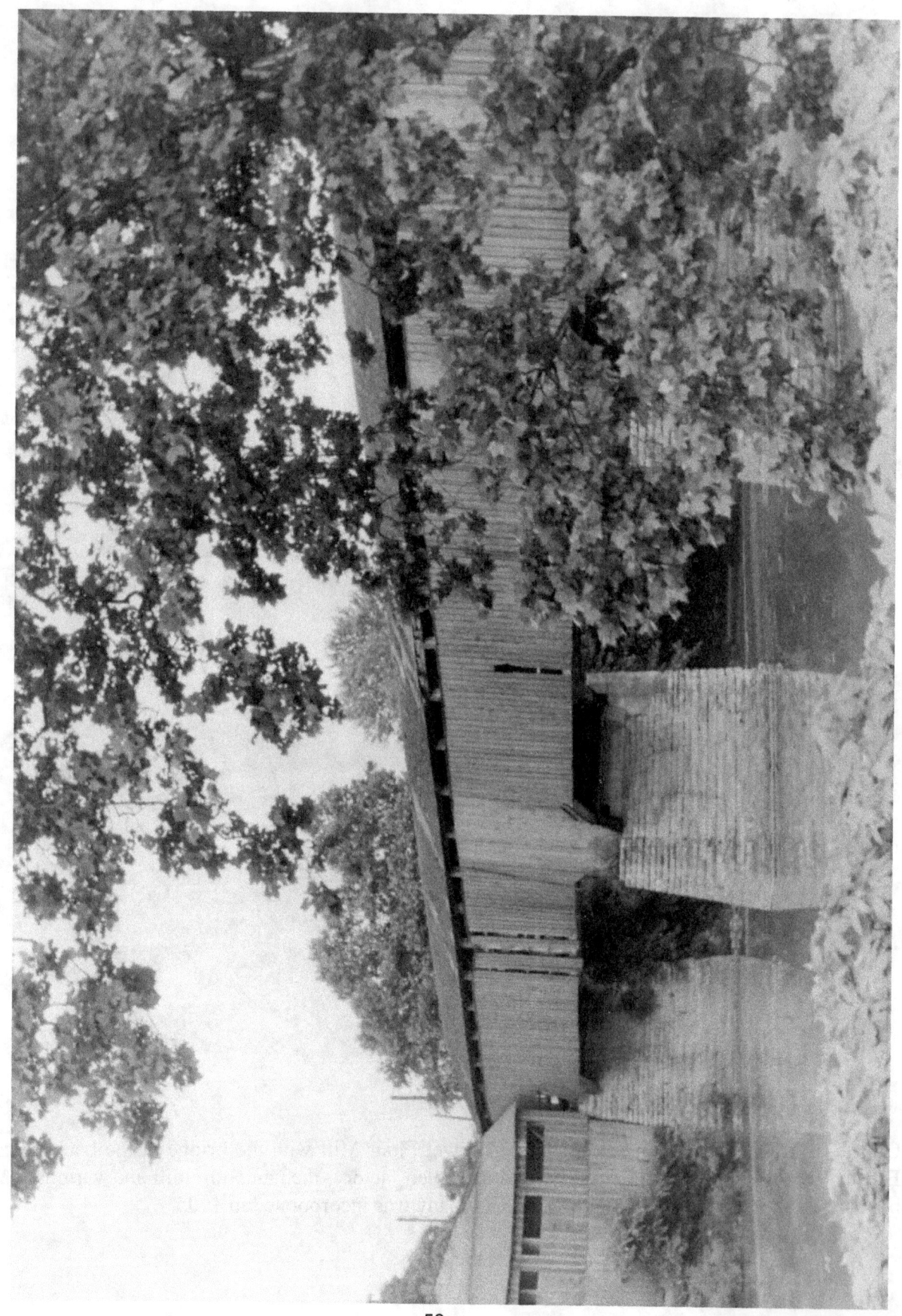

A testament to the bridge's strength, it withstood many floods such as this one in 1909.

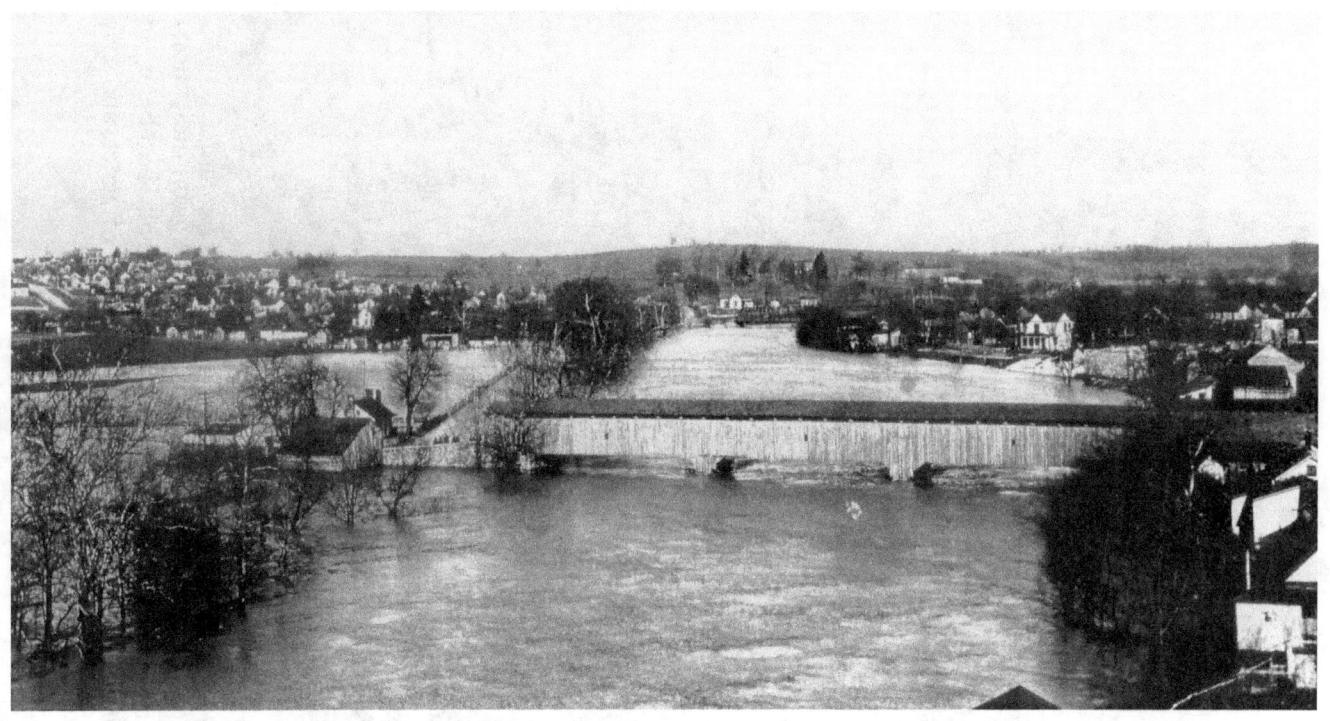

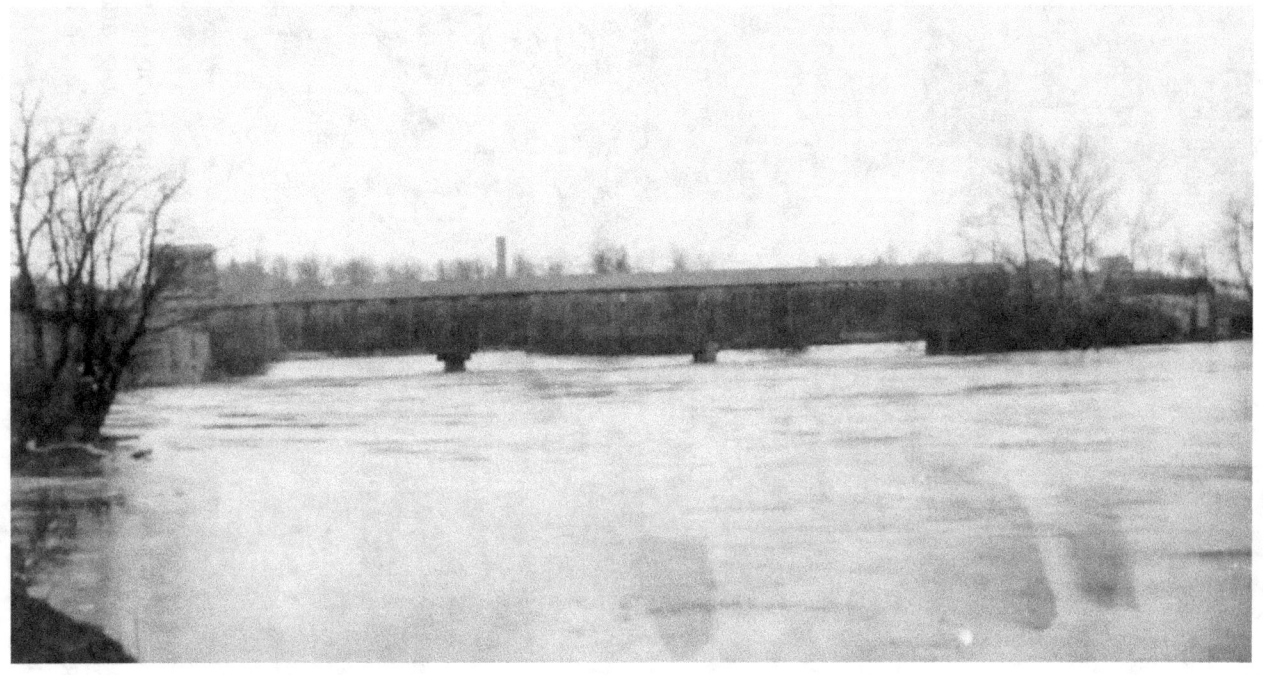

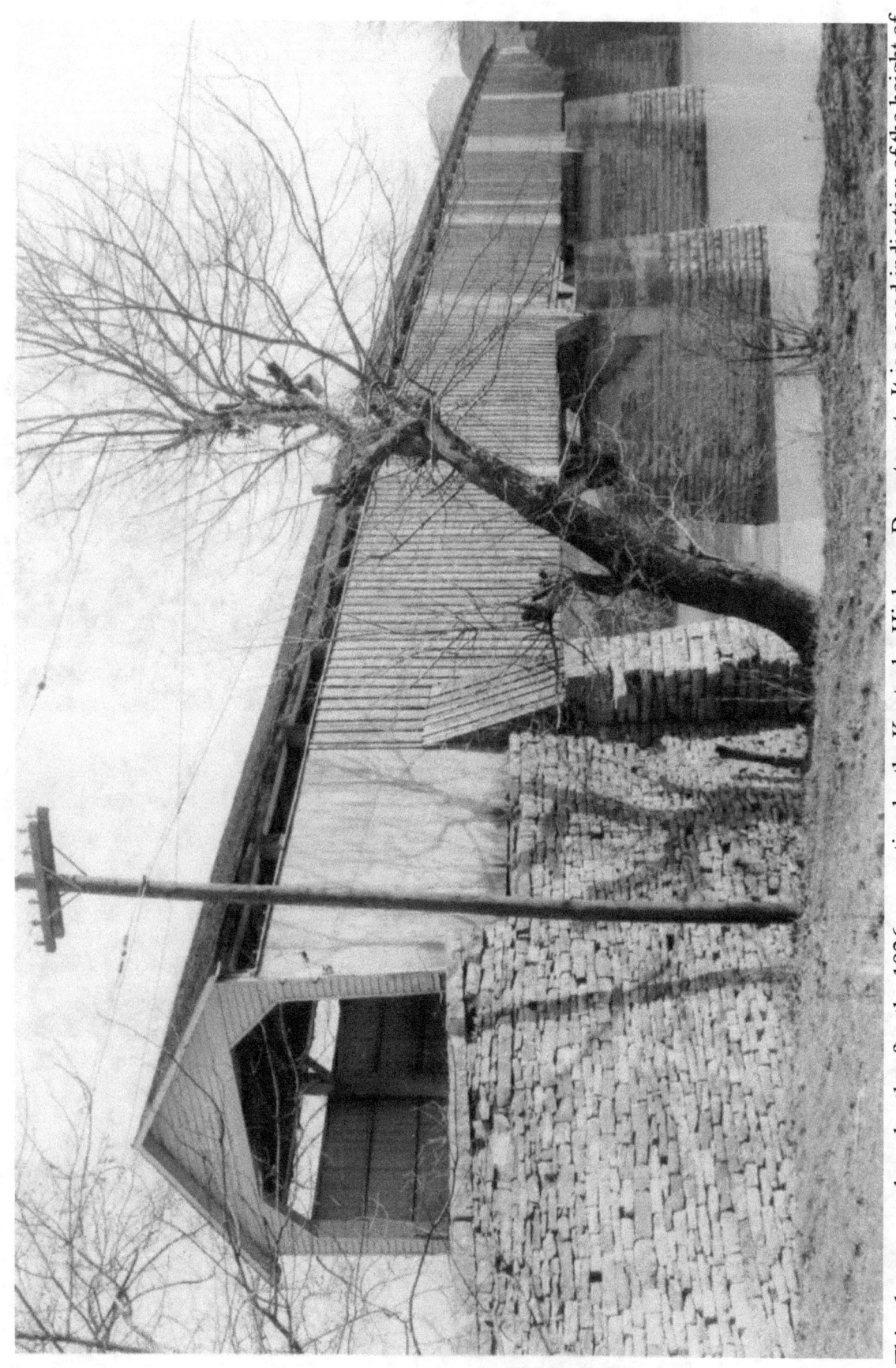

This photo was taken shortly after the 1926 renovation by the Kentucky Highway Department. It is a good indication of the height of the original dry stacked stone wing walls and the stone and mortar piers. (The concrete reinforcements had been added to the "ice breakers" near the top of each of the piers at a later date.) The piers stood in approximately three feet of water, and rose seventeen feet above the waterline.

After 107 years of continuous service the bridge was declared structurally inadequate and County Road Engineer W. H. Criswell blocked the portals to the bridge under orders of the Harrison County Fiscal Court and the Cynthiana Board of Commissioners. This began the debate of whether the bridge should be repaired and reopened, be preserved but remain closed or to be replaced all together.

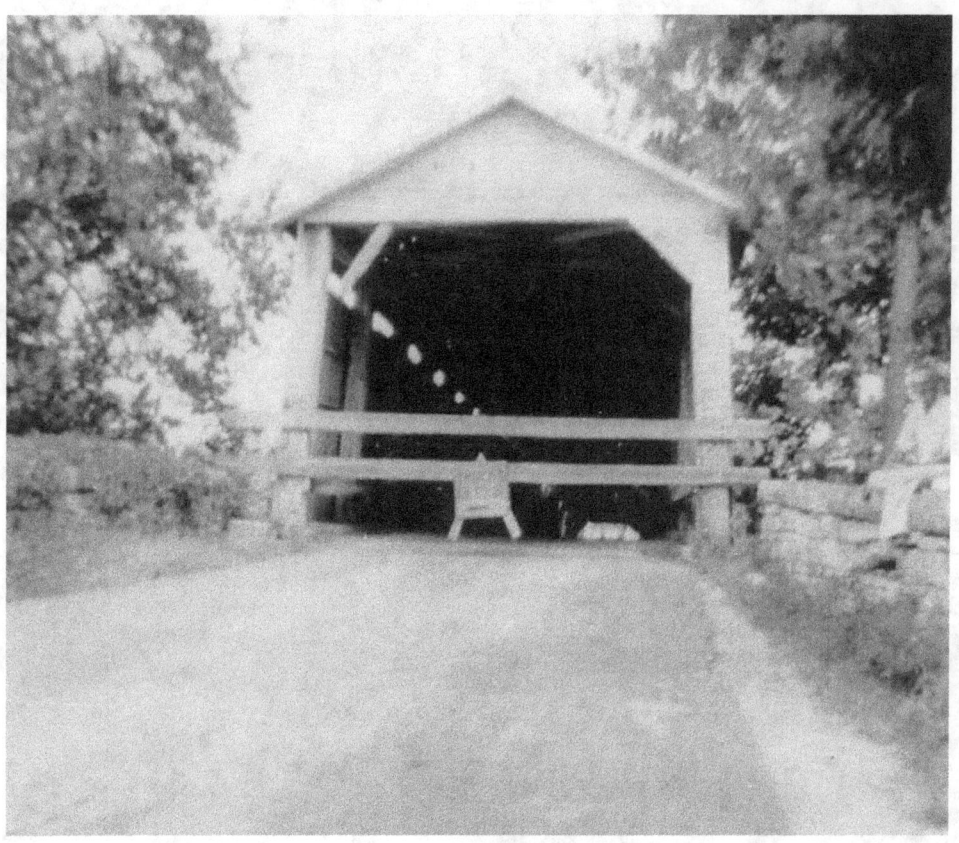

Lois Taylor Dennis poses outside the closed bridge.

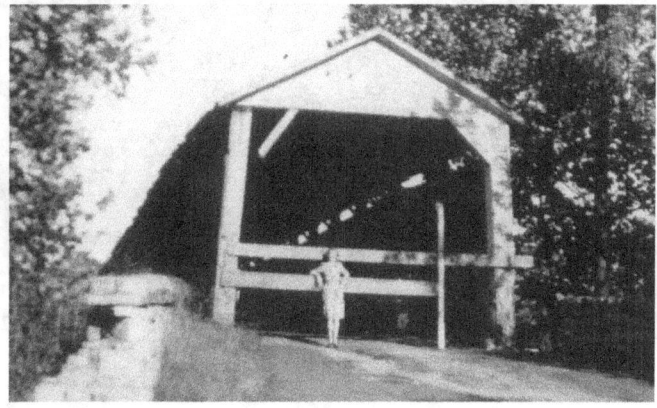

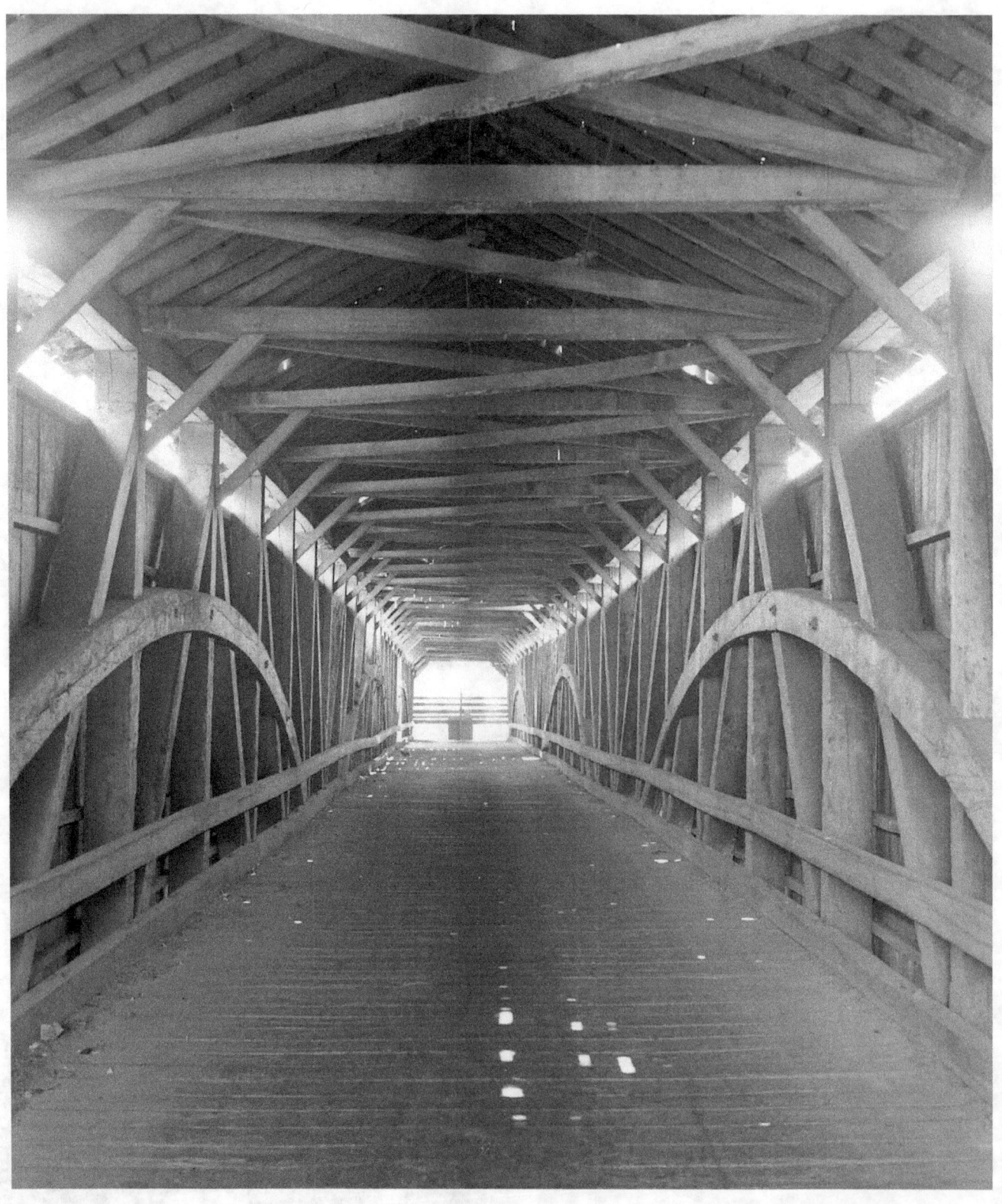

This photo of the graceful triple arches of the Burr Arch truss was taken on June 25, 1944, a few days after the bridge was closed.

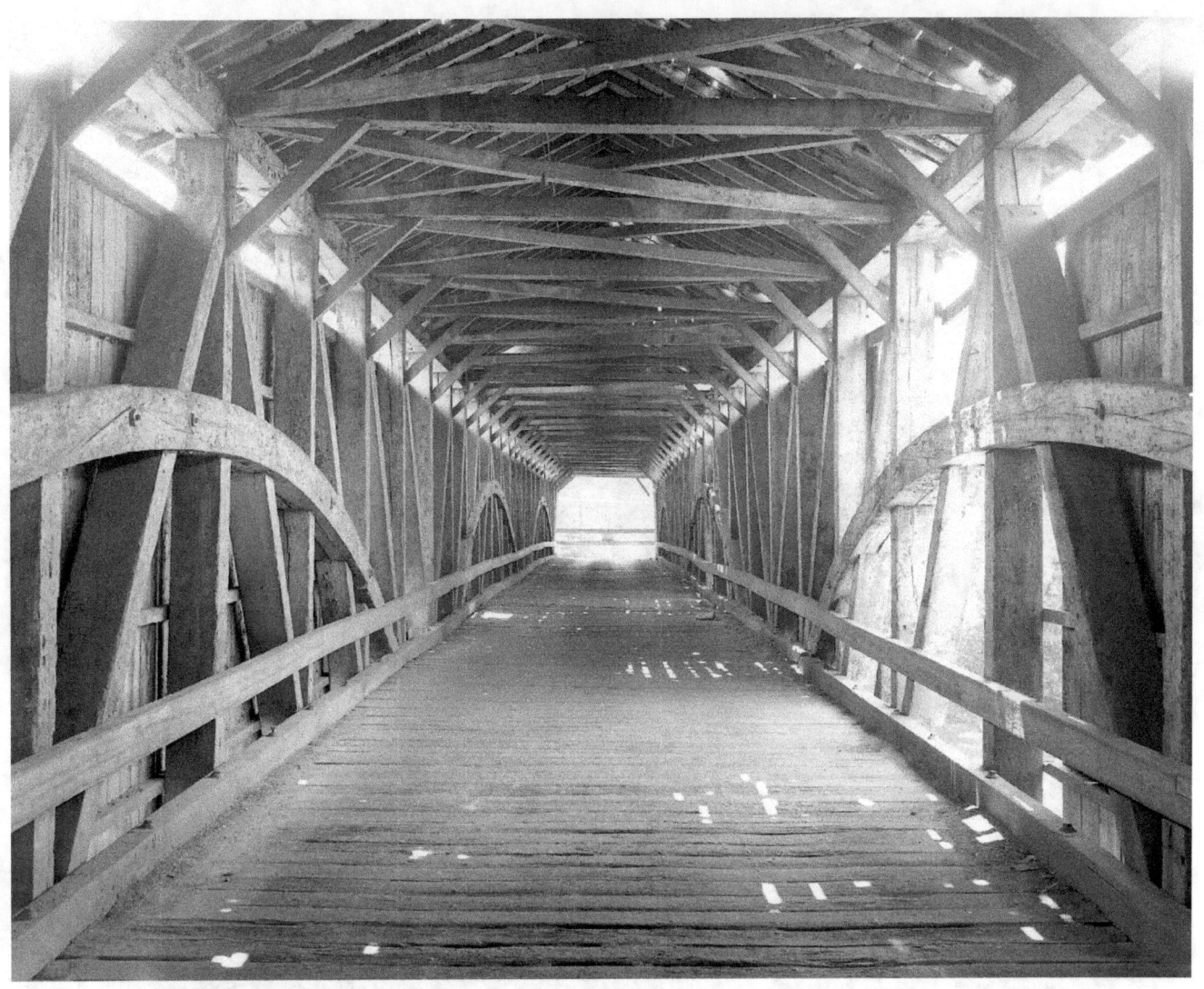

After the bridge was closed to traffic many seemed certain that the bridge would be preserved due to its historical significance and prominent role in the Battle of Cynthiana during the Civil War. Many locals expressed their opinion that without the bridge their community would become just another nondescript town someone would encounter on their journey, pass through without stopping and not remember. They said the bridge was a reason to stop and the tourism it brought, and would continue to bring, business to town.

Alas the rallies were to no avail and the demolition of the bridge began on May 17, 1946. The bridge was a victim of a lack of vision of the prosperity it would have brought to the area for many years and a lack of appreciation of its history.

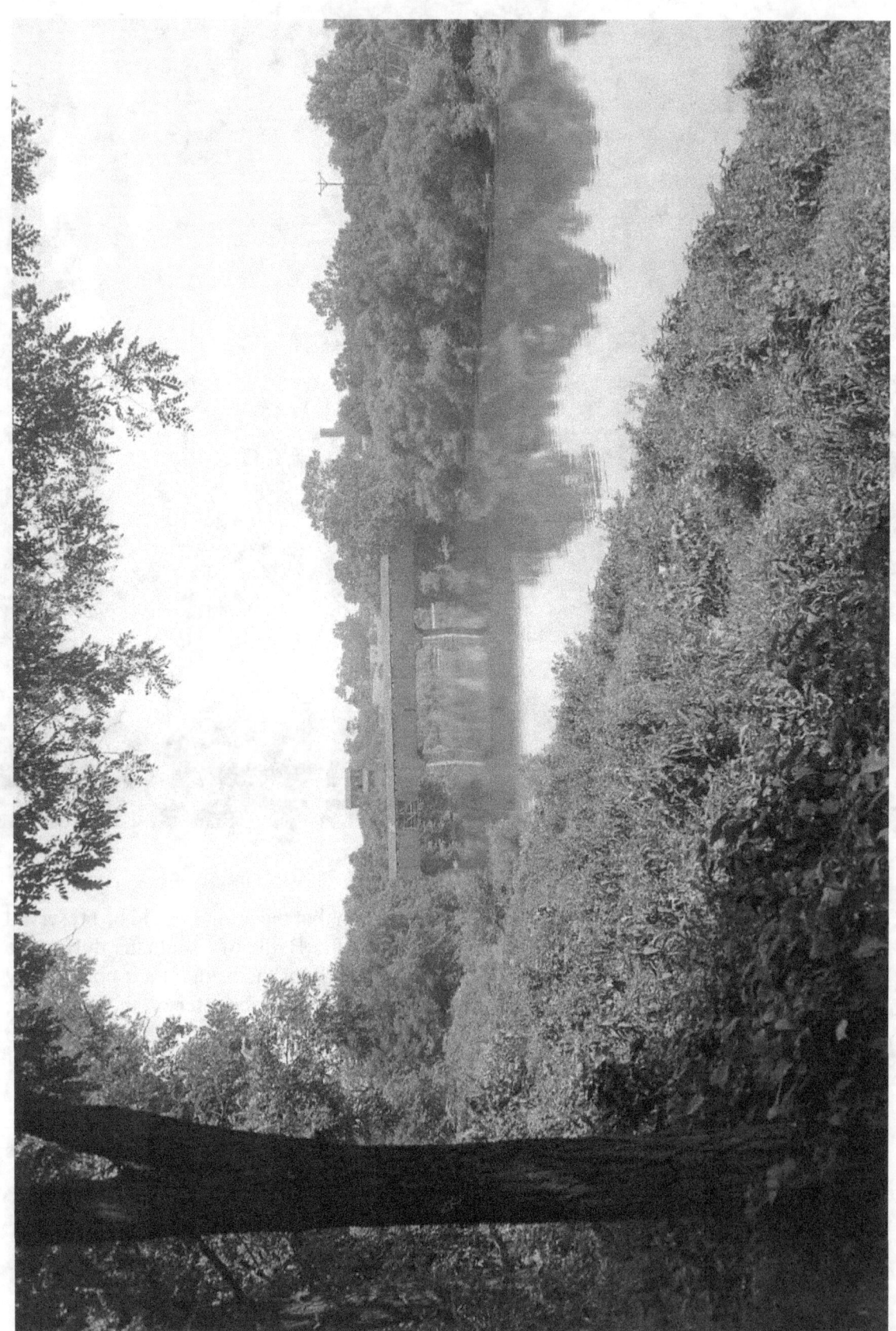

May 18,1946

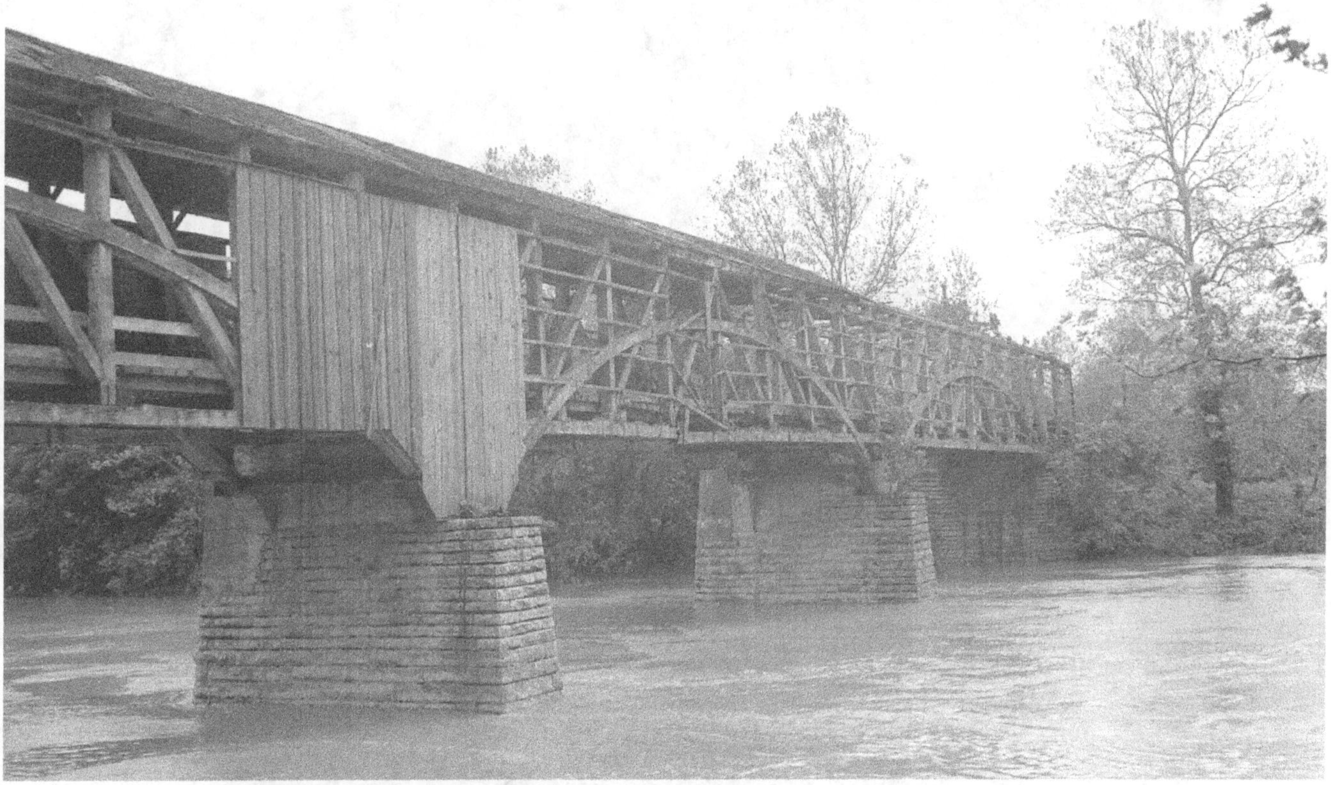

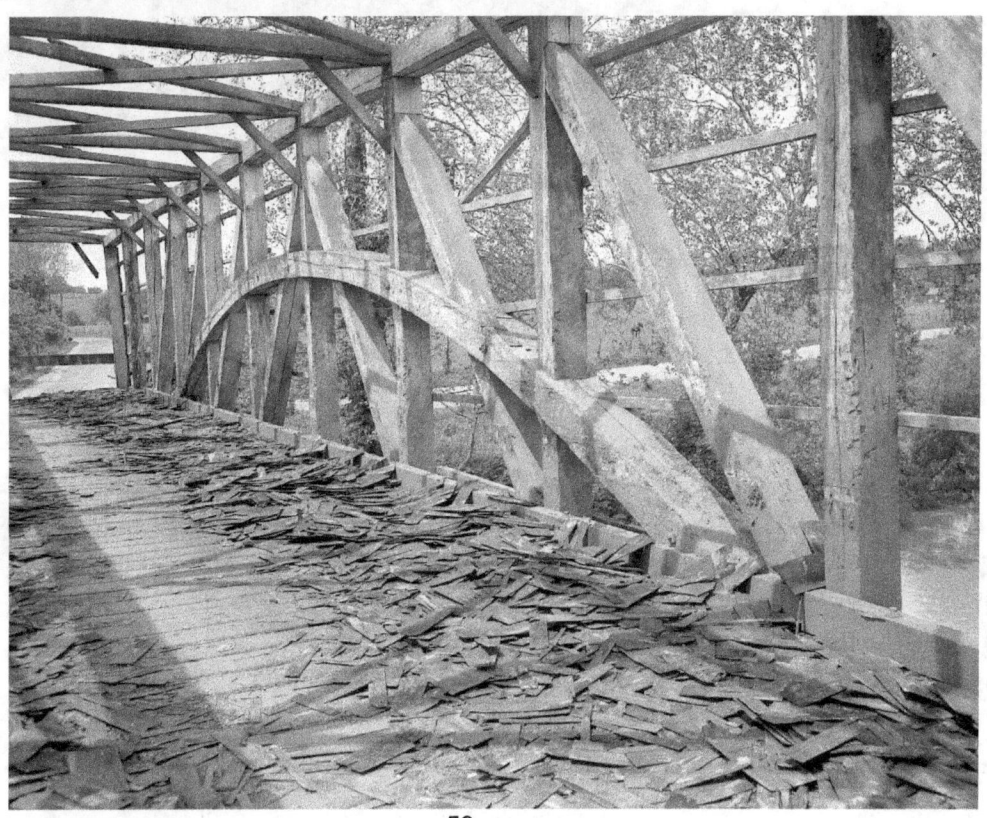

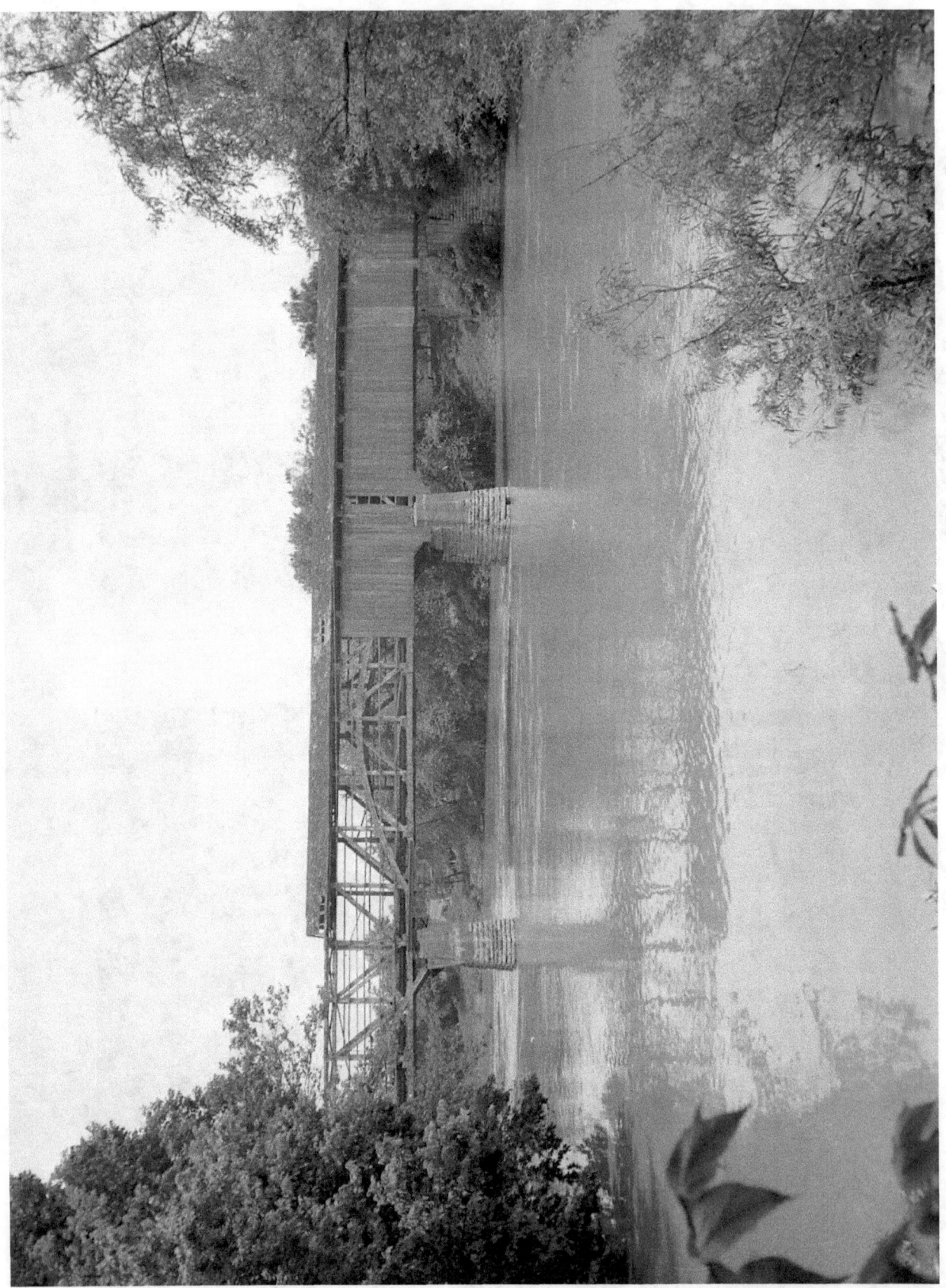

May 19, 1946

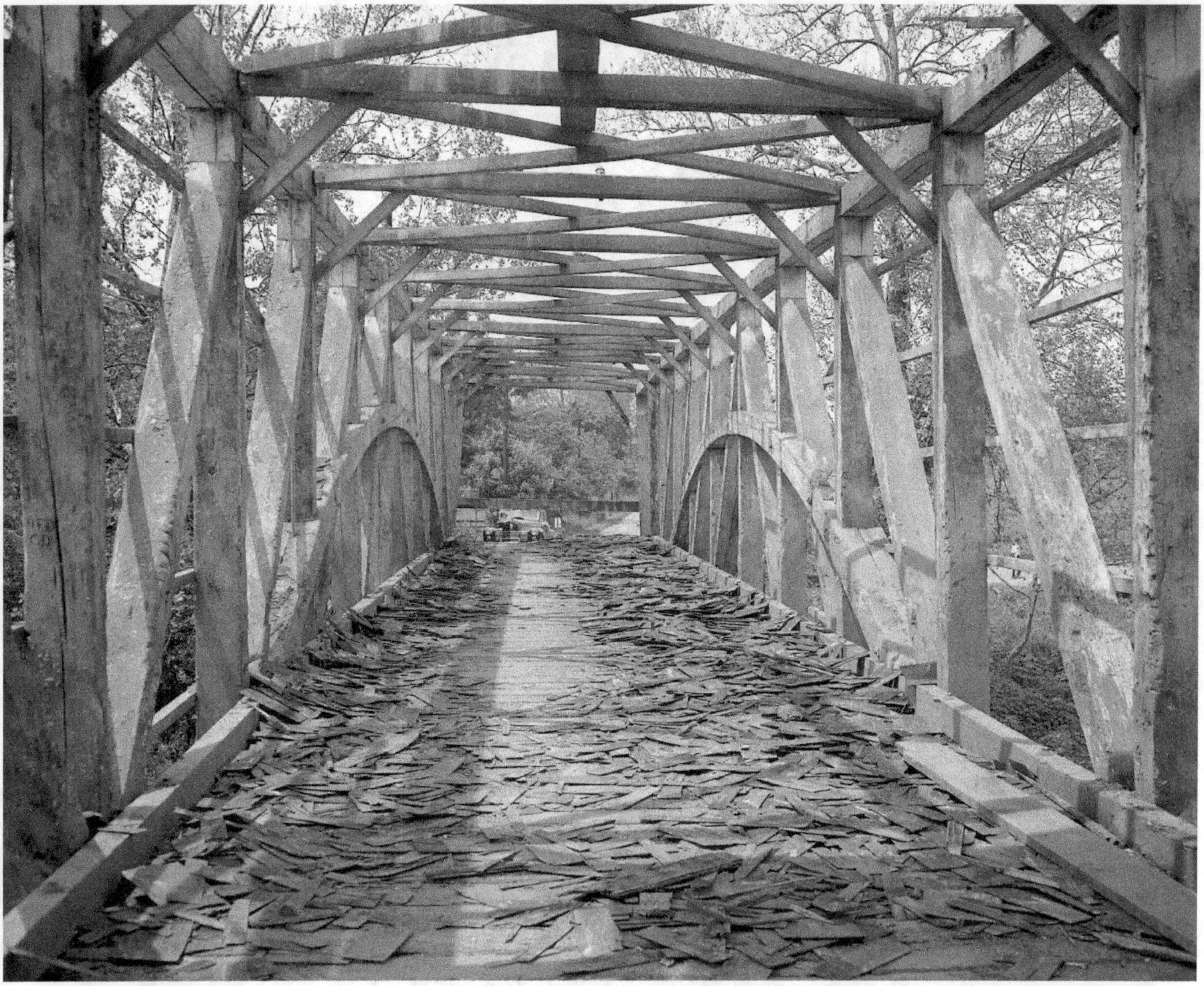

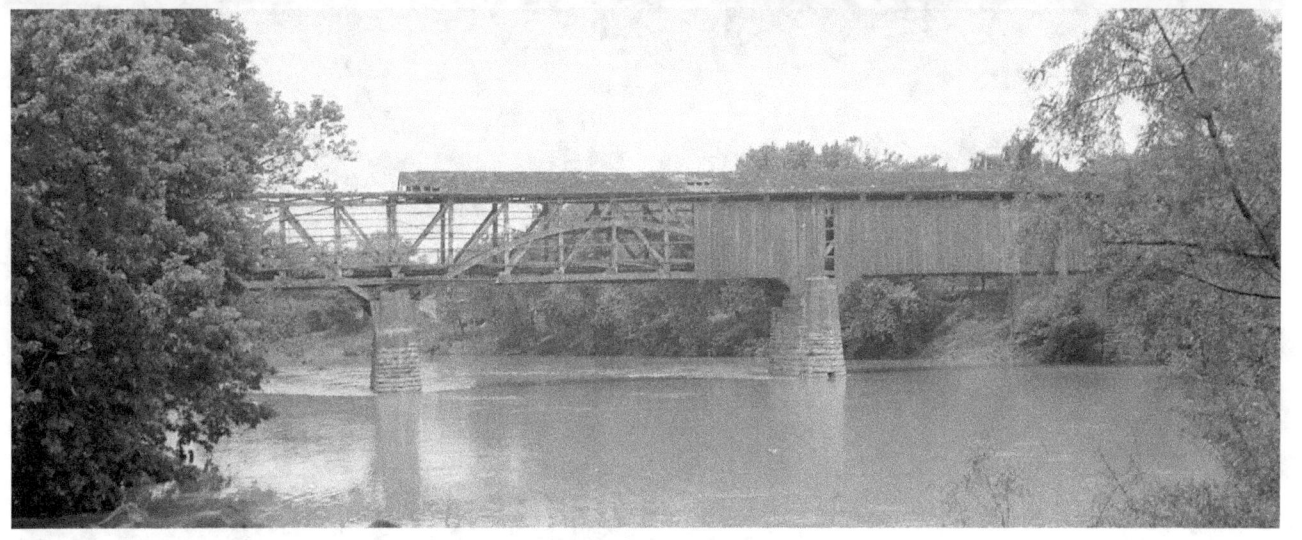

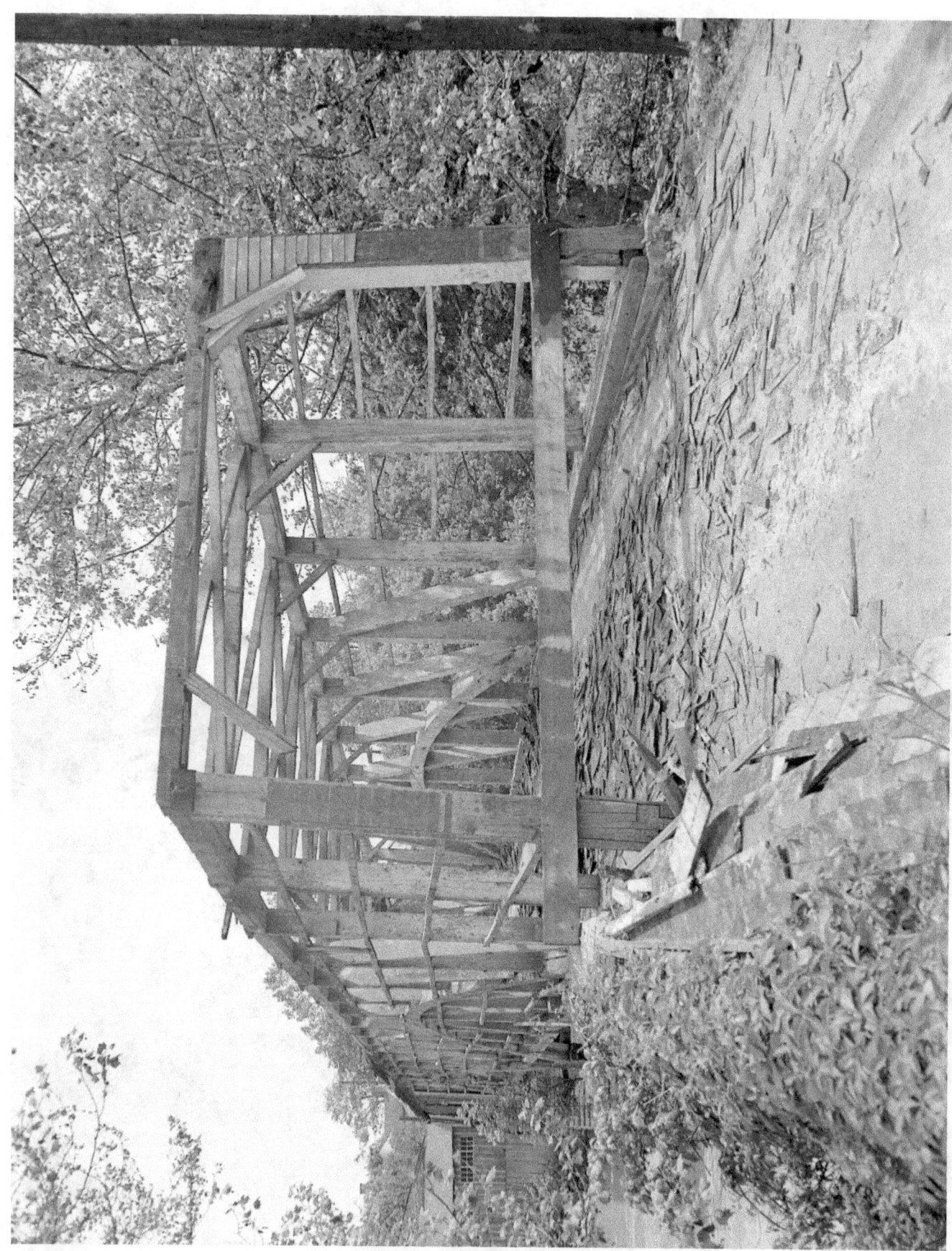

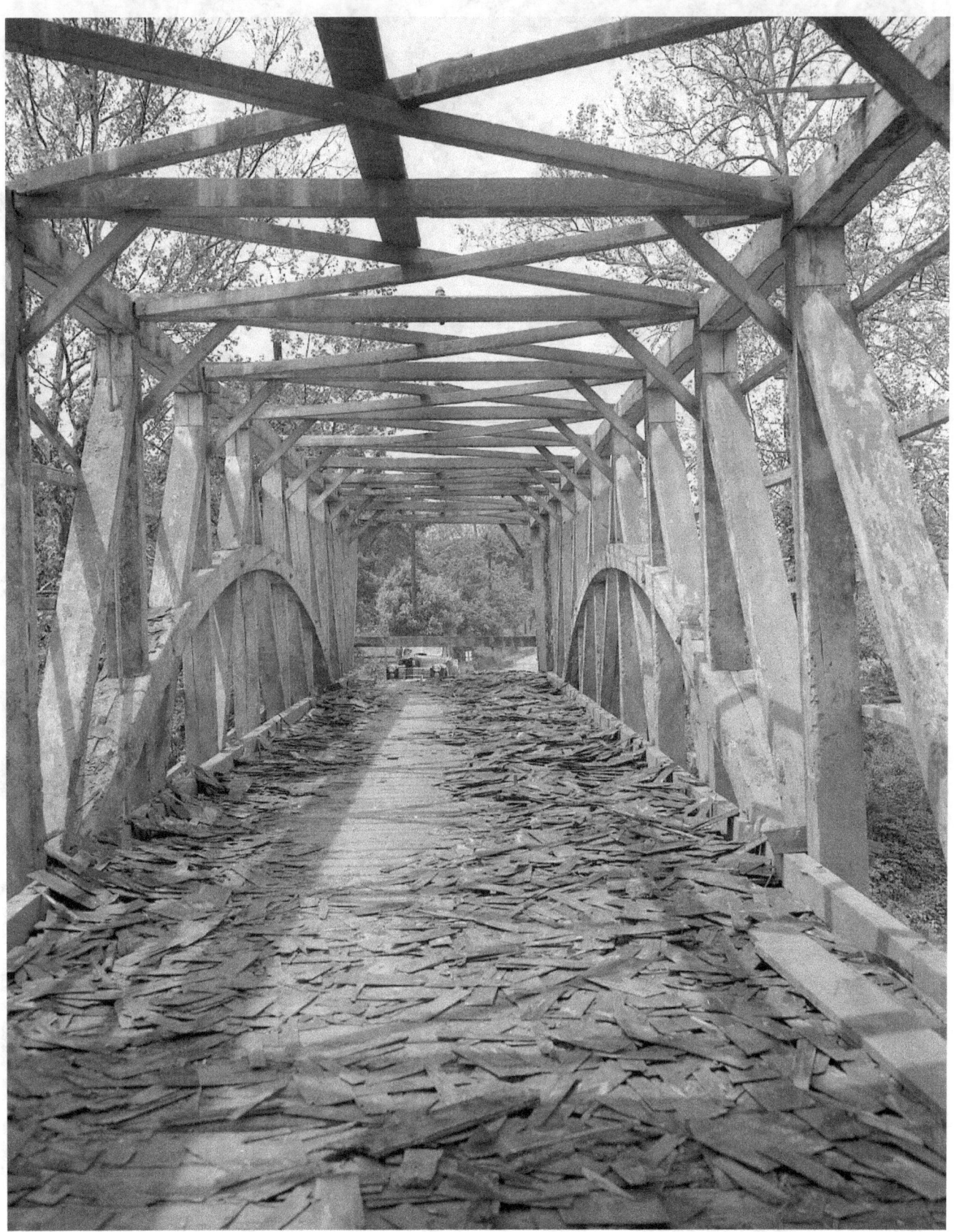

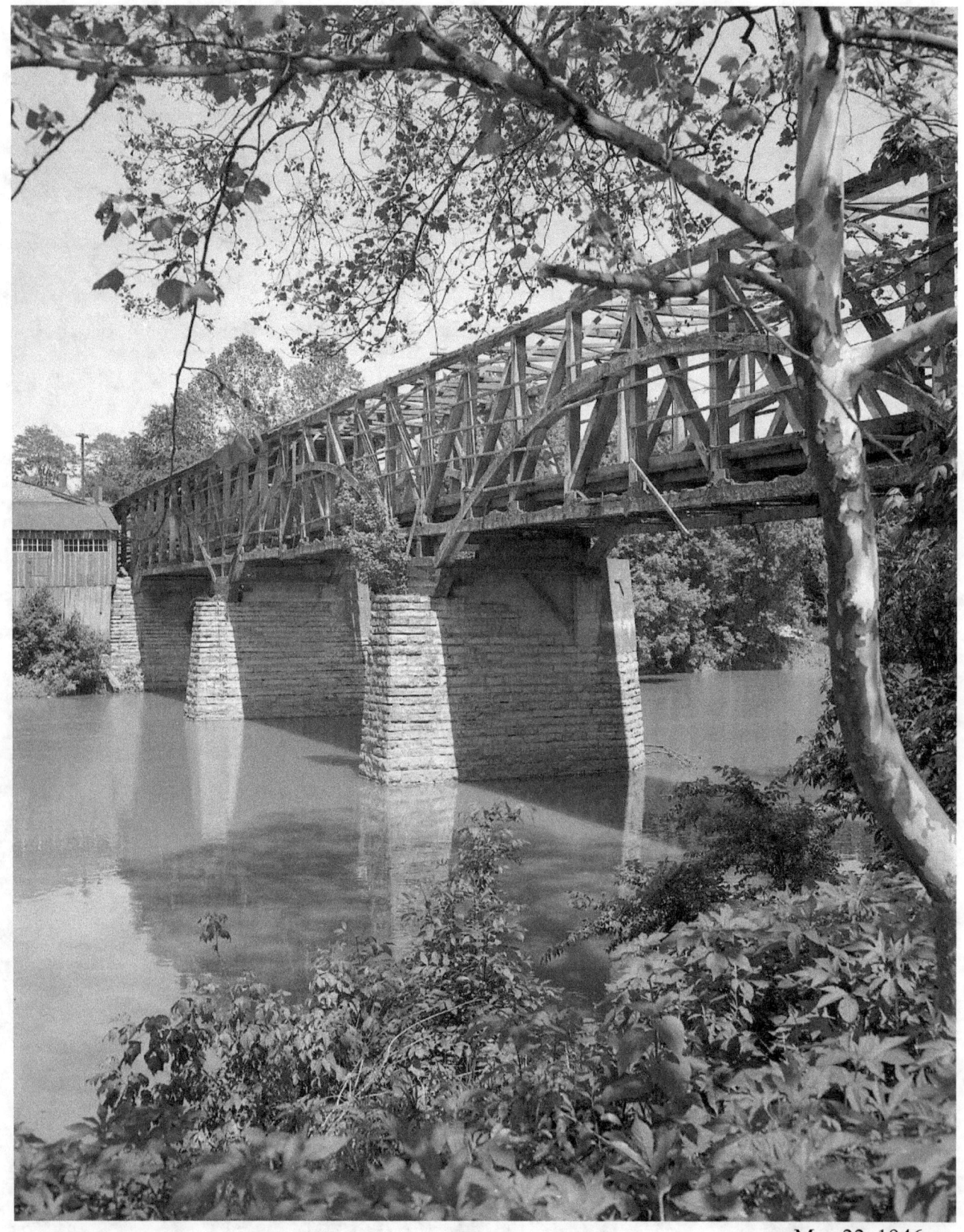

May 22, 1946

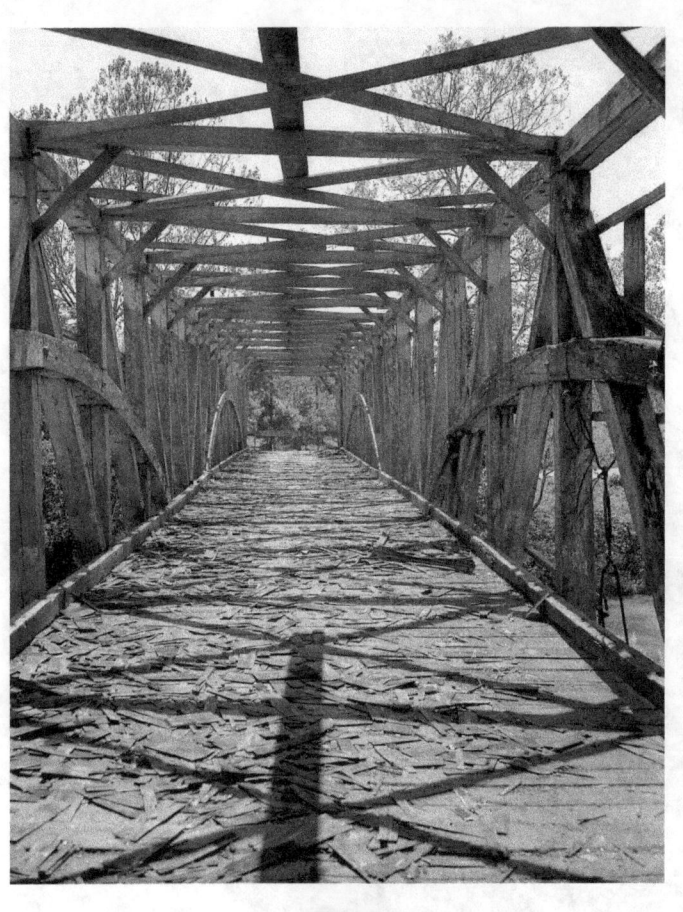

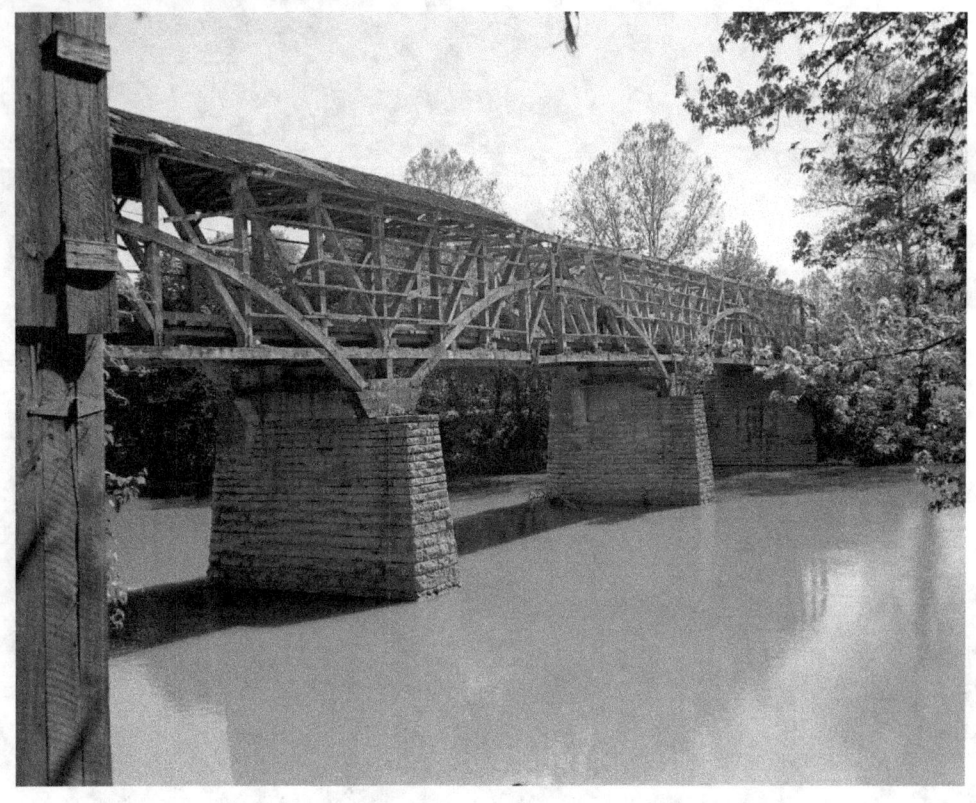

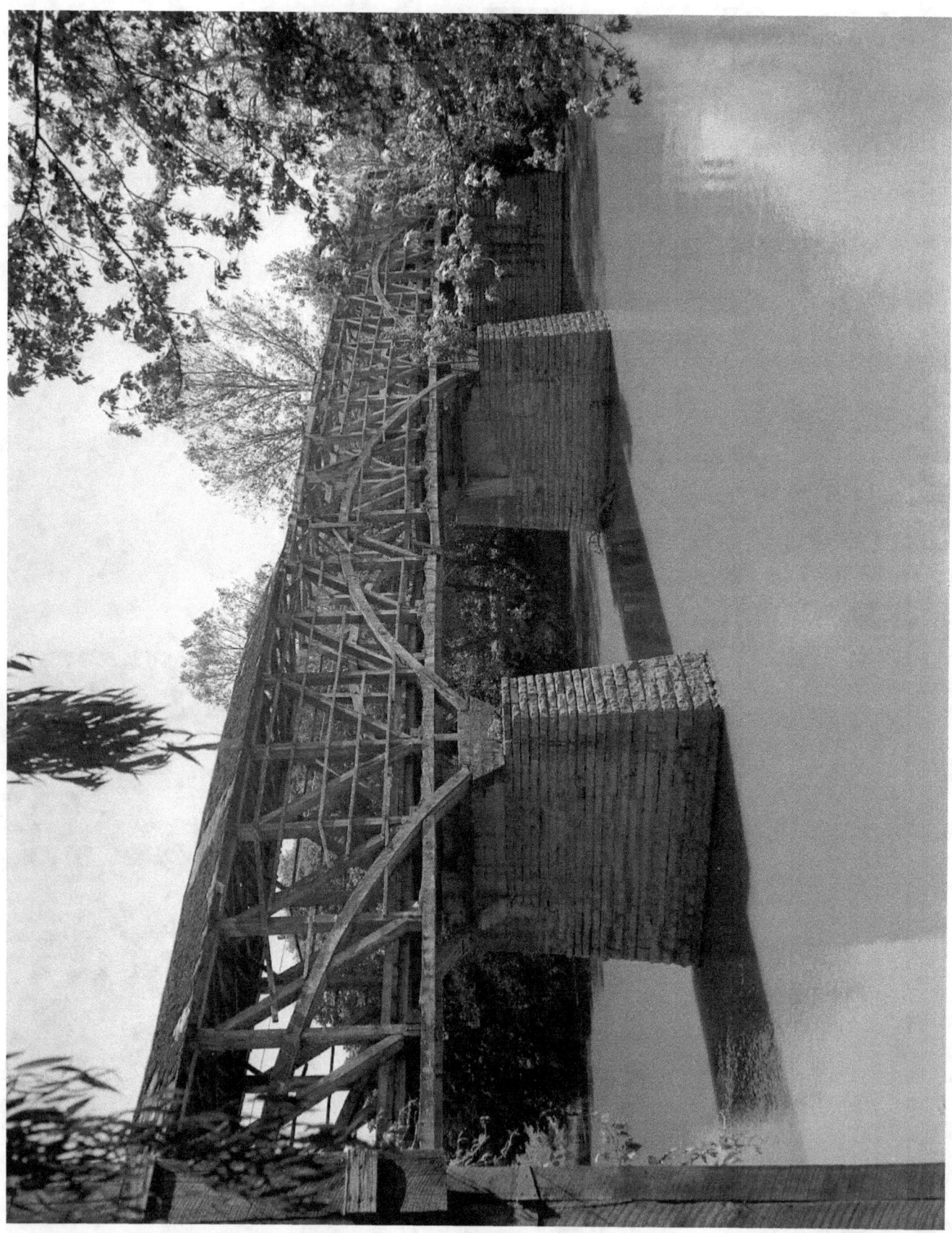

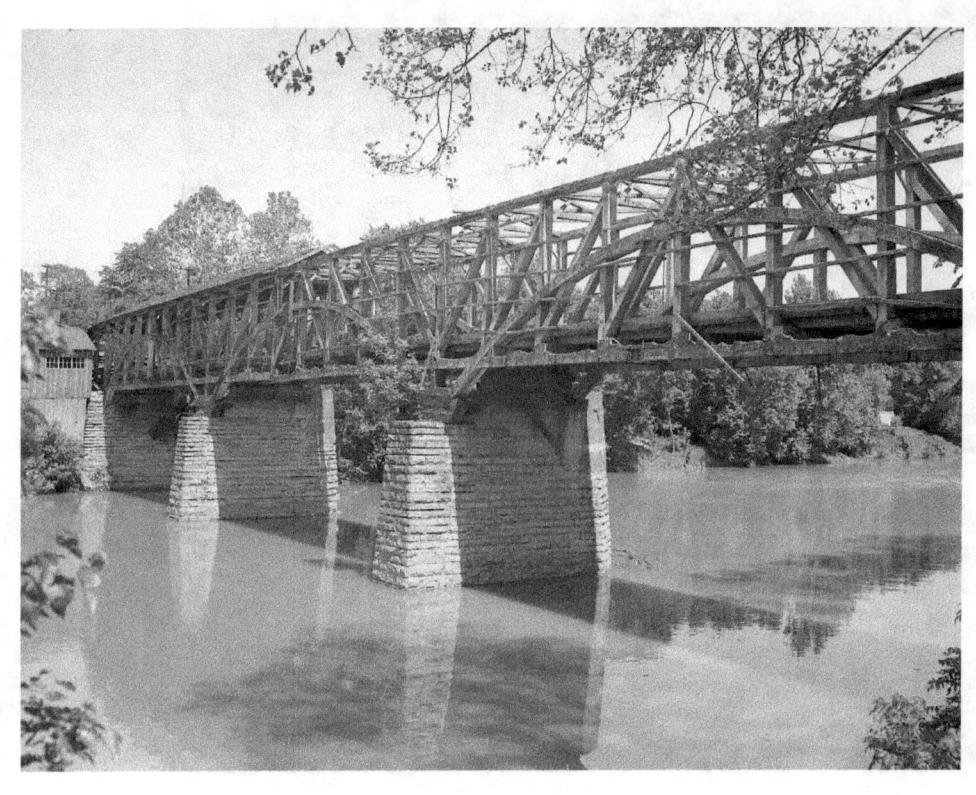

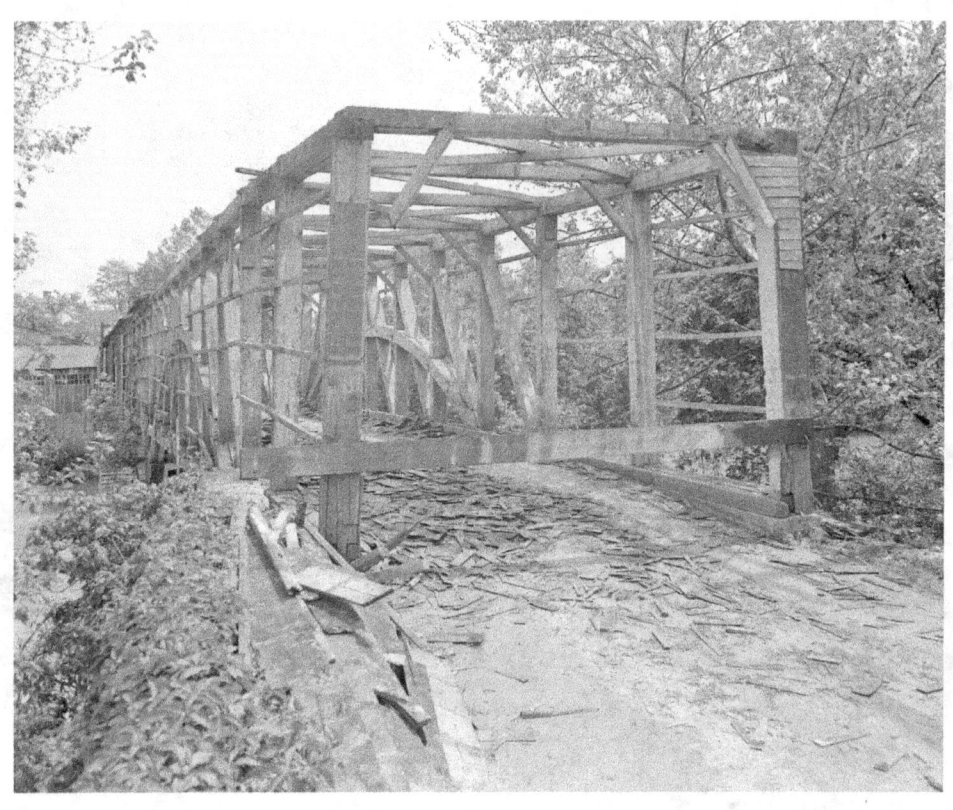

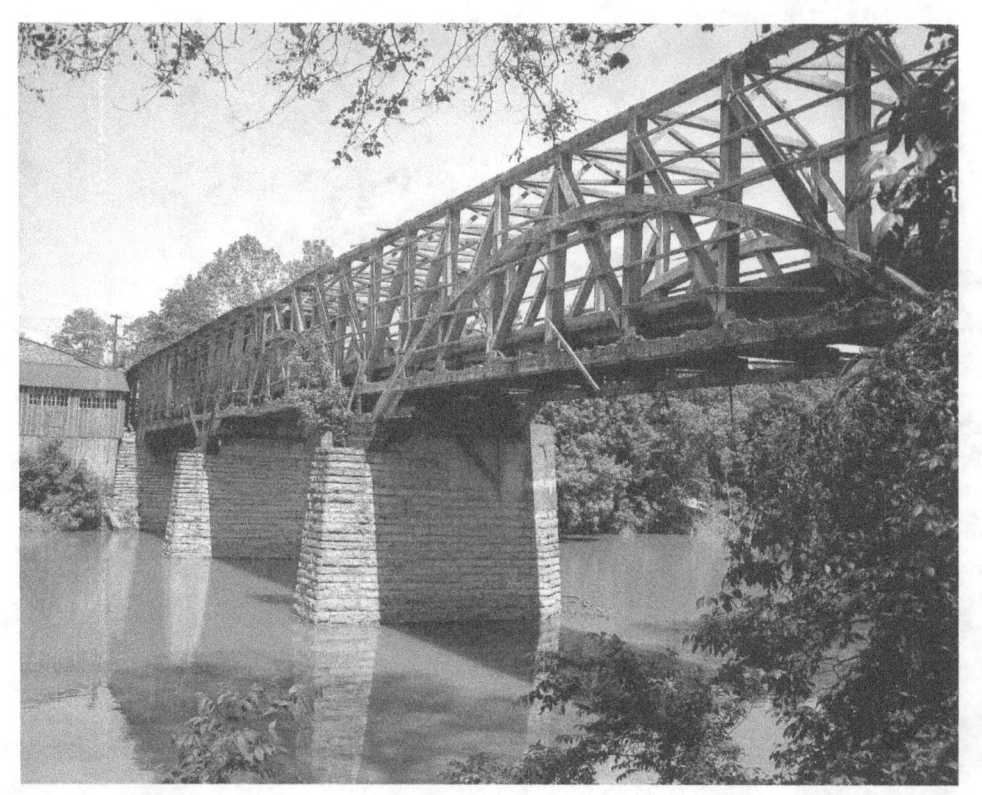

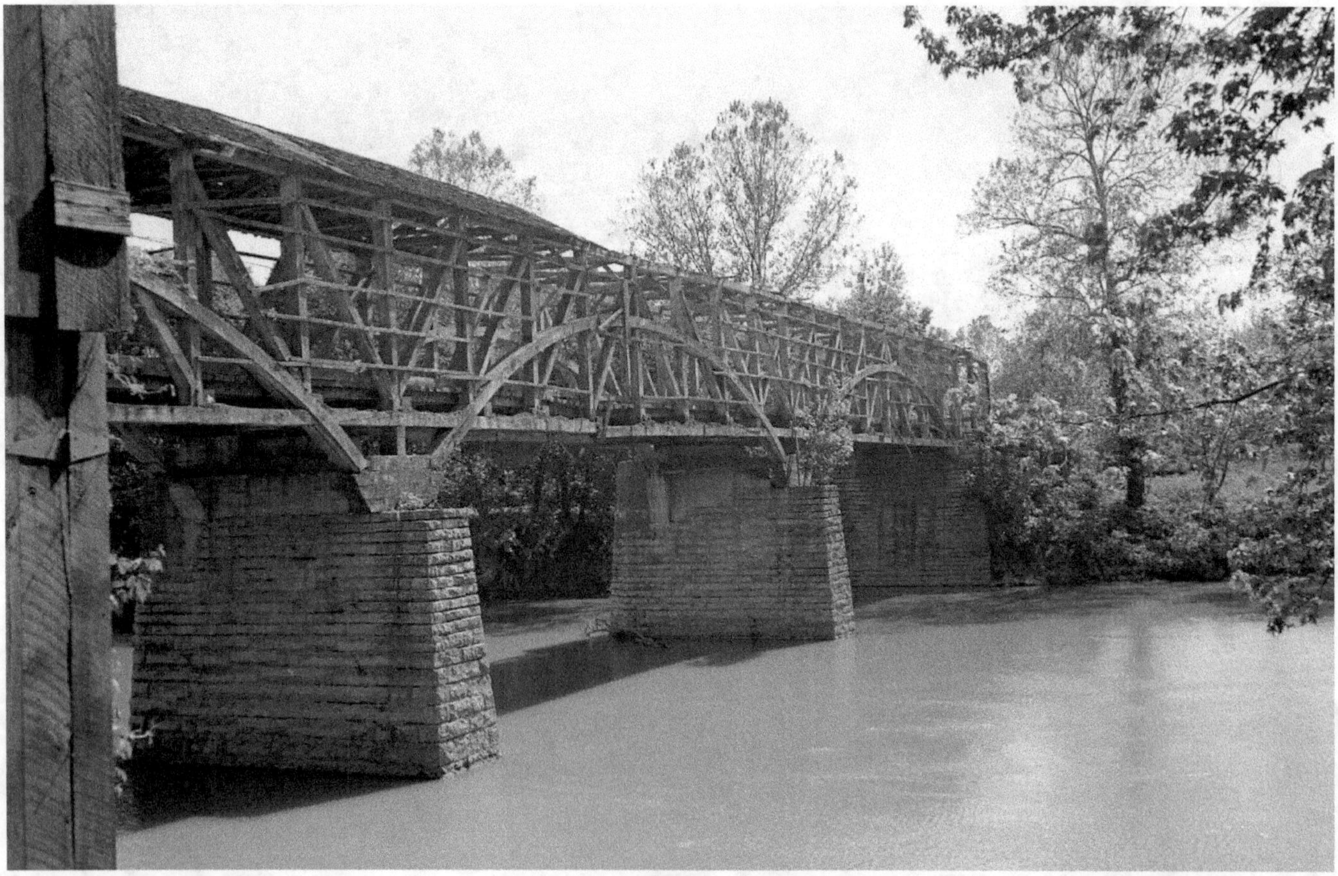

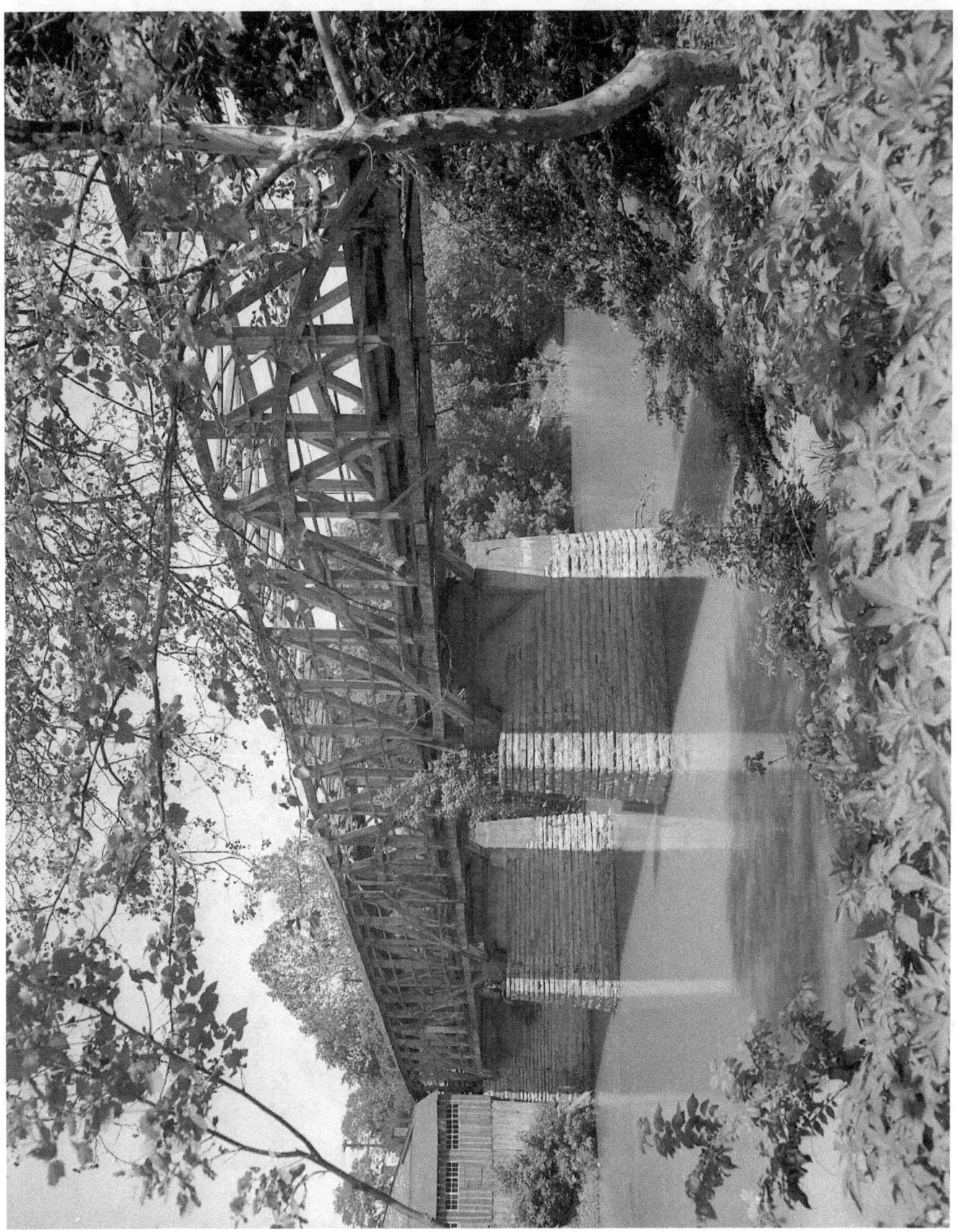

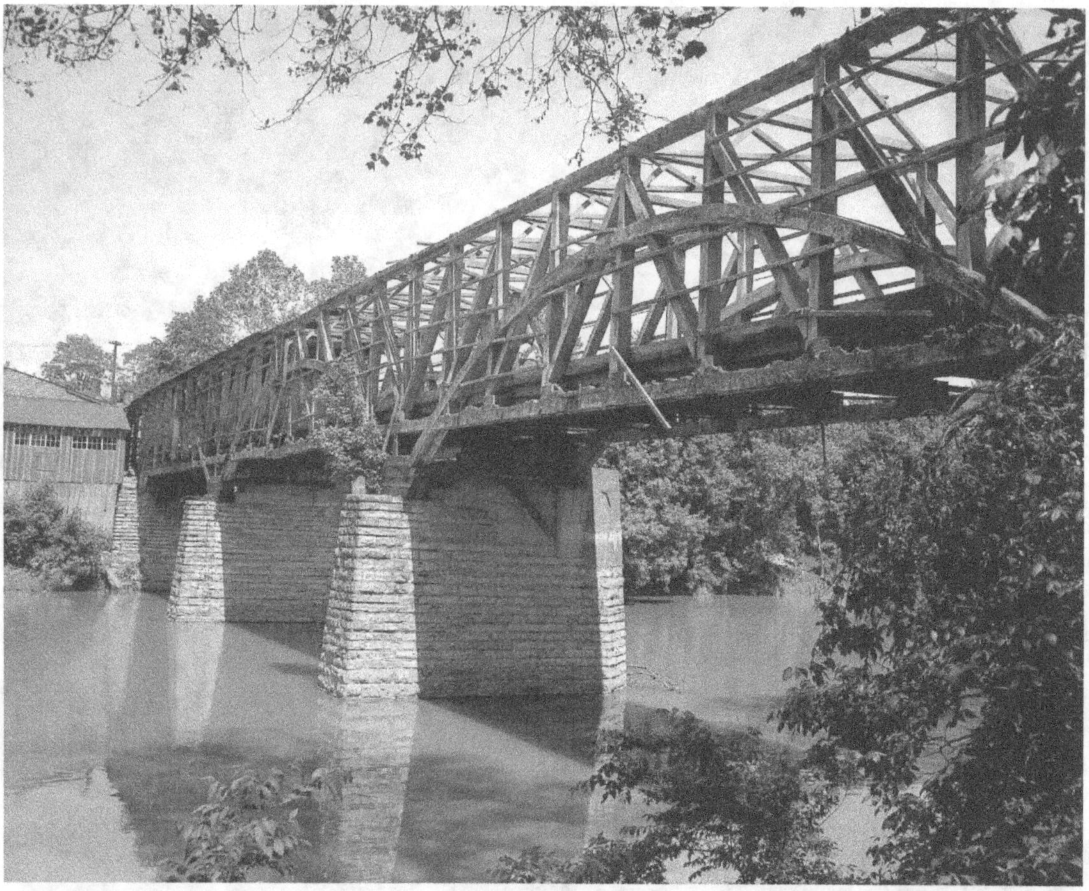

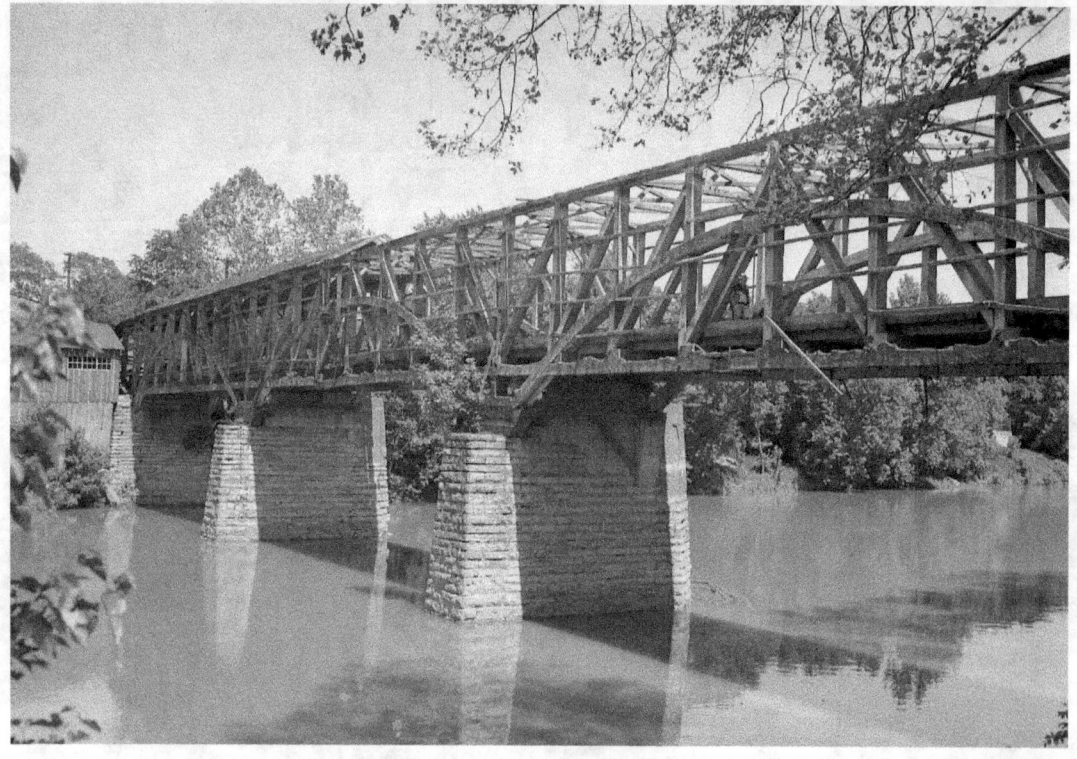

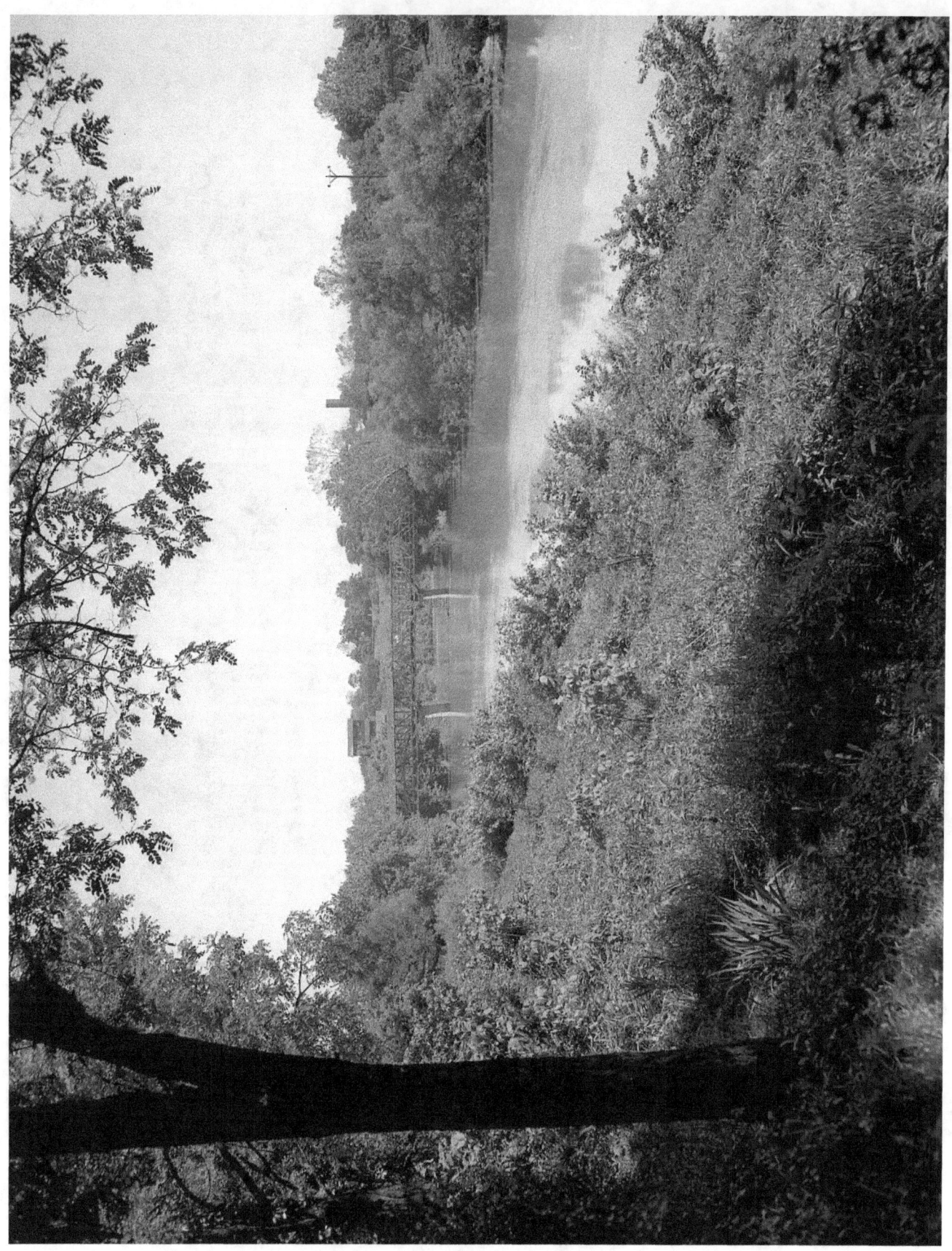

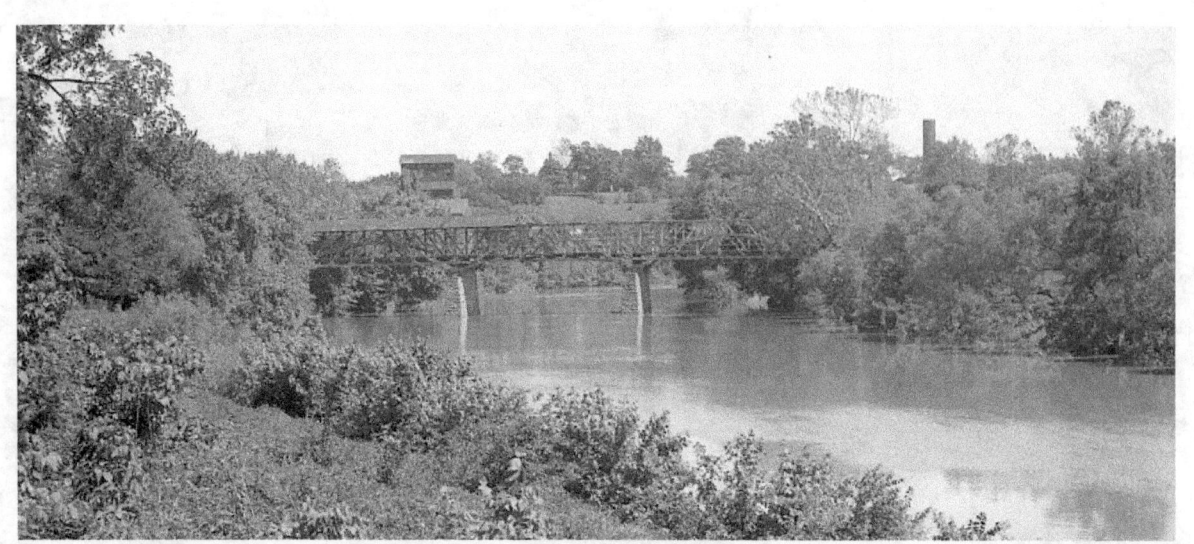

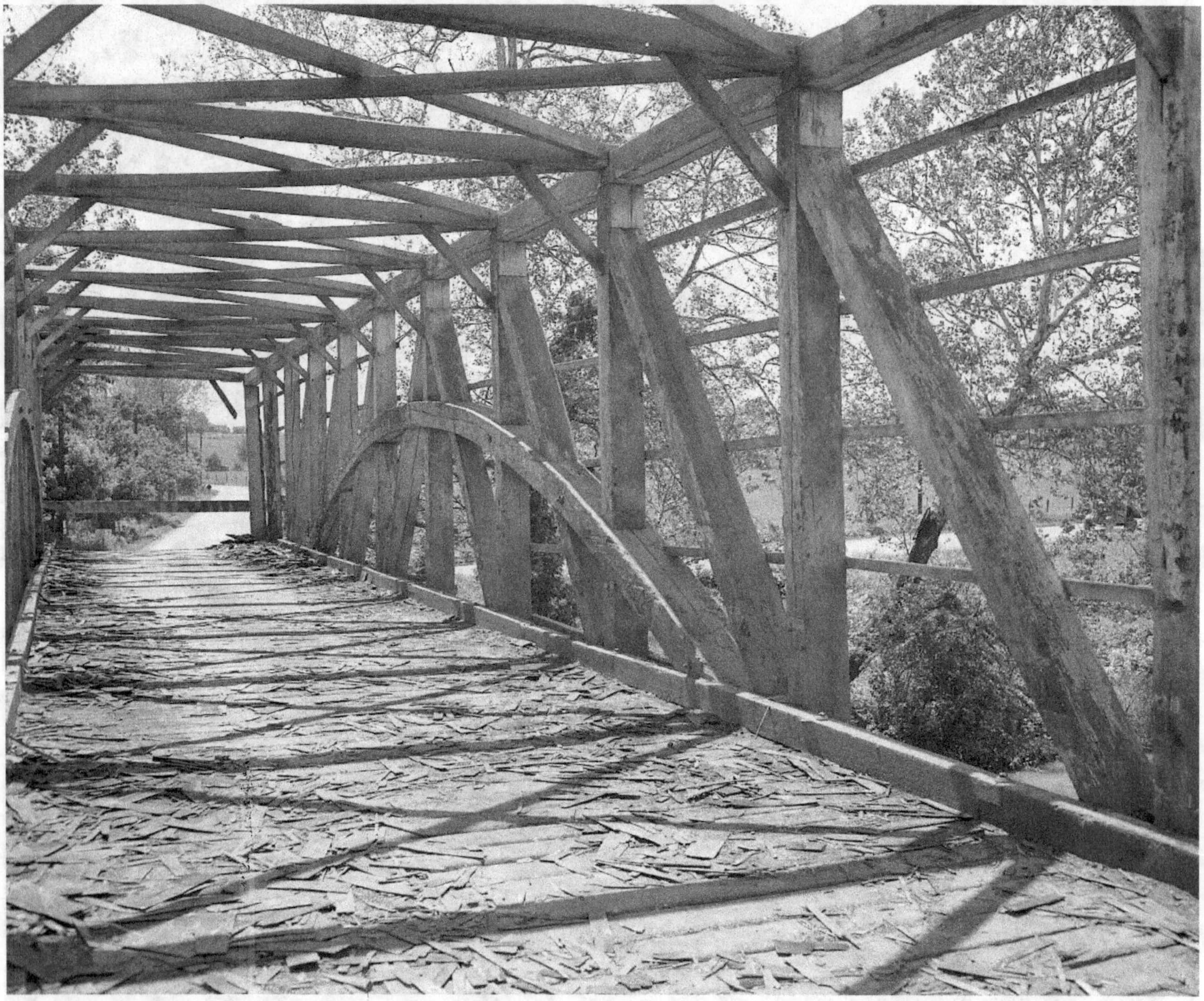

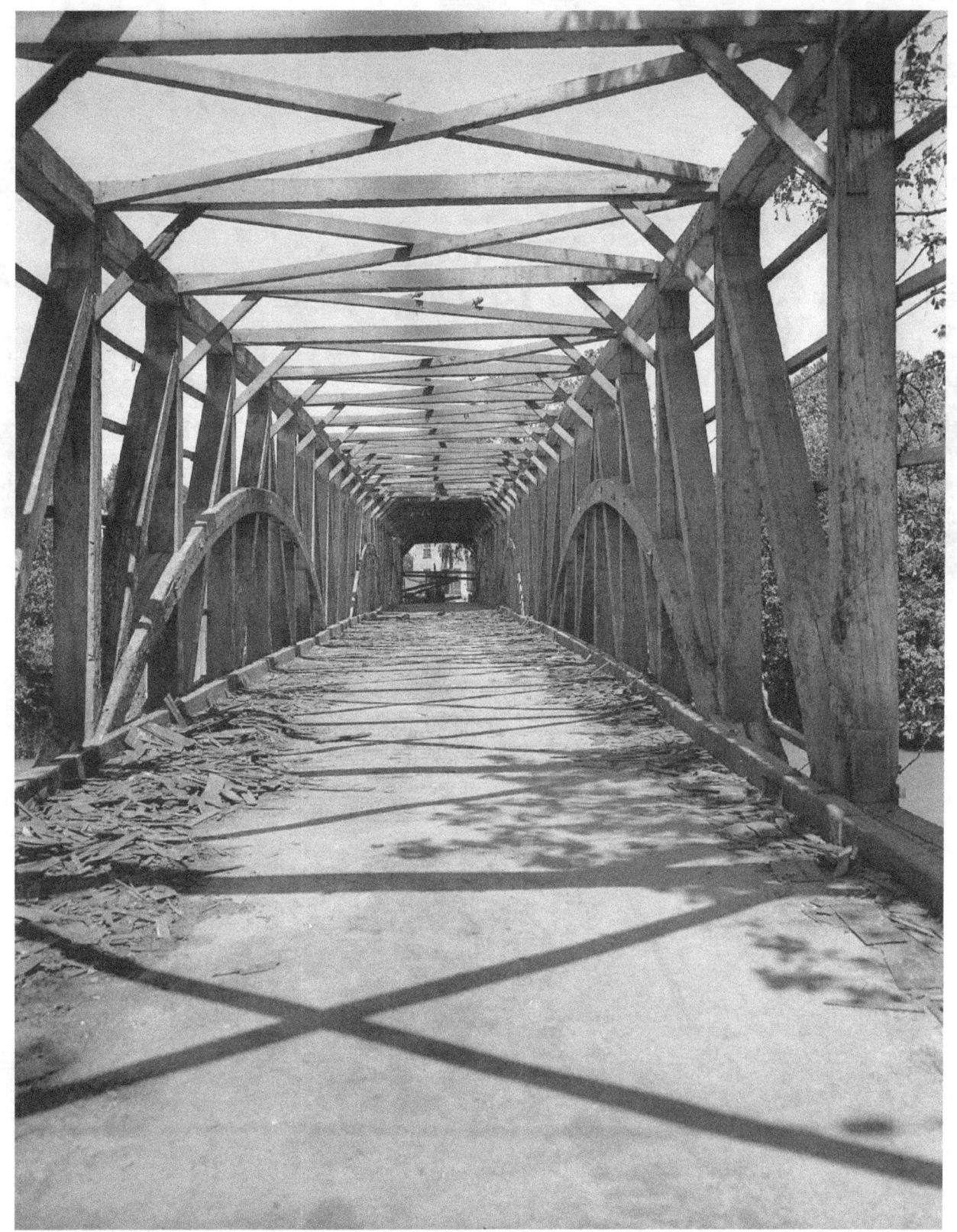

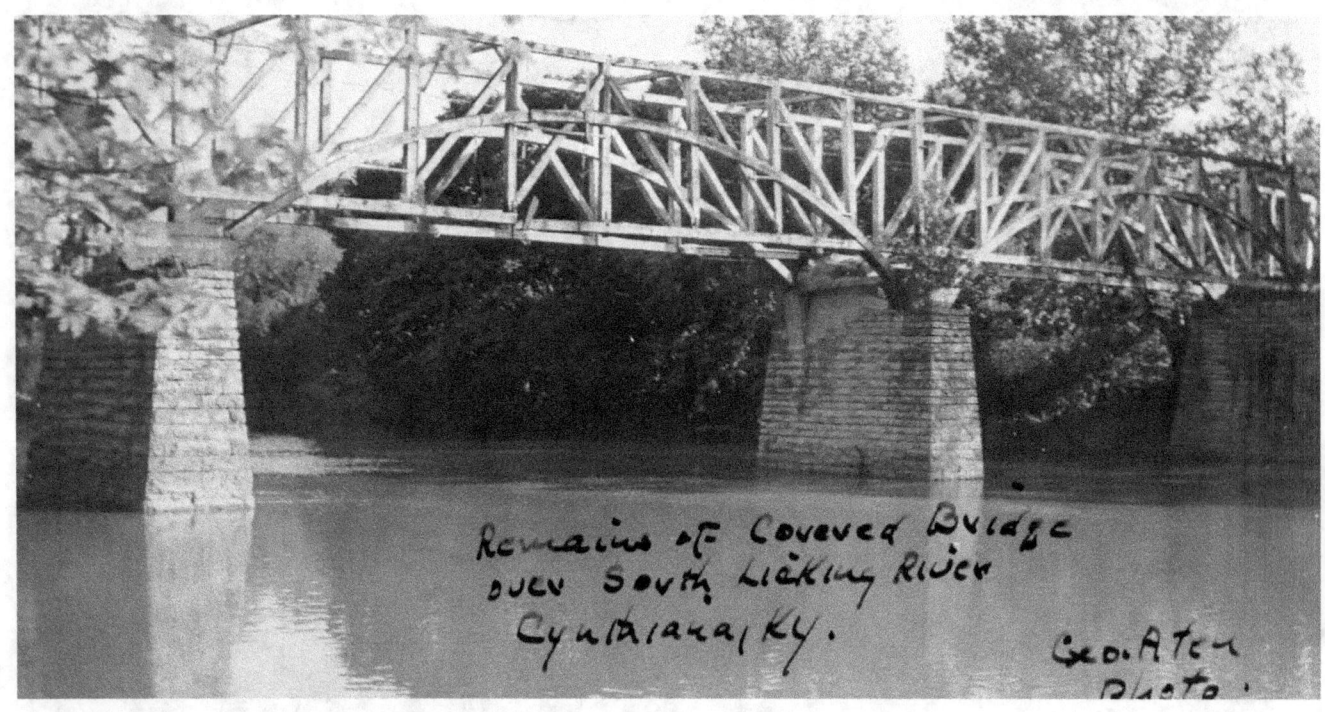

Remains of Covered Bridge
over South Licking River
Cynthiana, Ky.

Geo. Aten
Photo.

For reasons unknown on the afternoon of December 18, 1946 a 1936 Ford attempted to cross the floorless bridge. The car was occupied by three men and two teenage girls. Clarence Moore, 23, was the only survivor of the accident. Daisy Mitchell, 17, Mildred Young, 17, and Jesse Darnell, 34, died at the scene while Raymond Moore, 24, died in the hospital the next day.

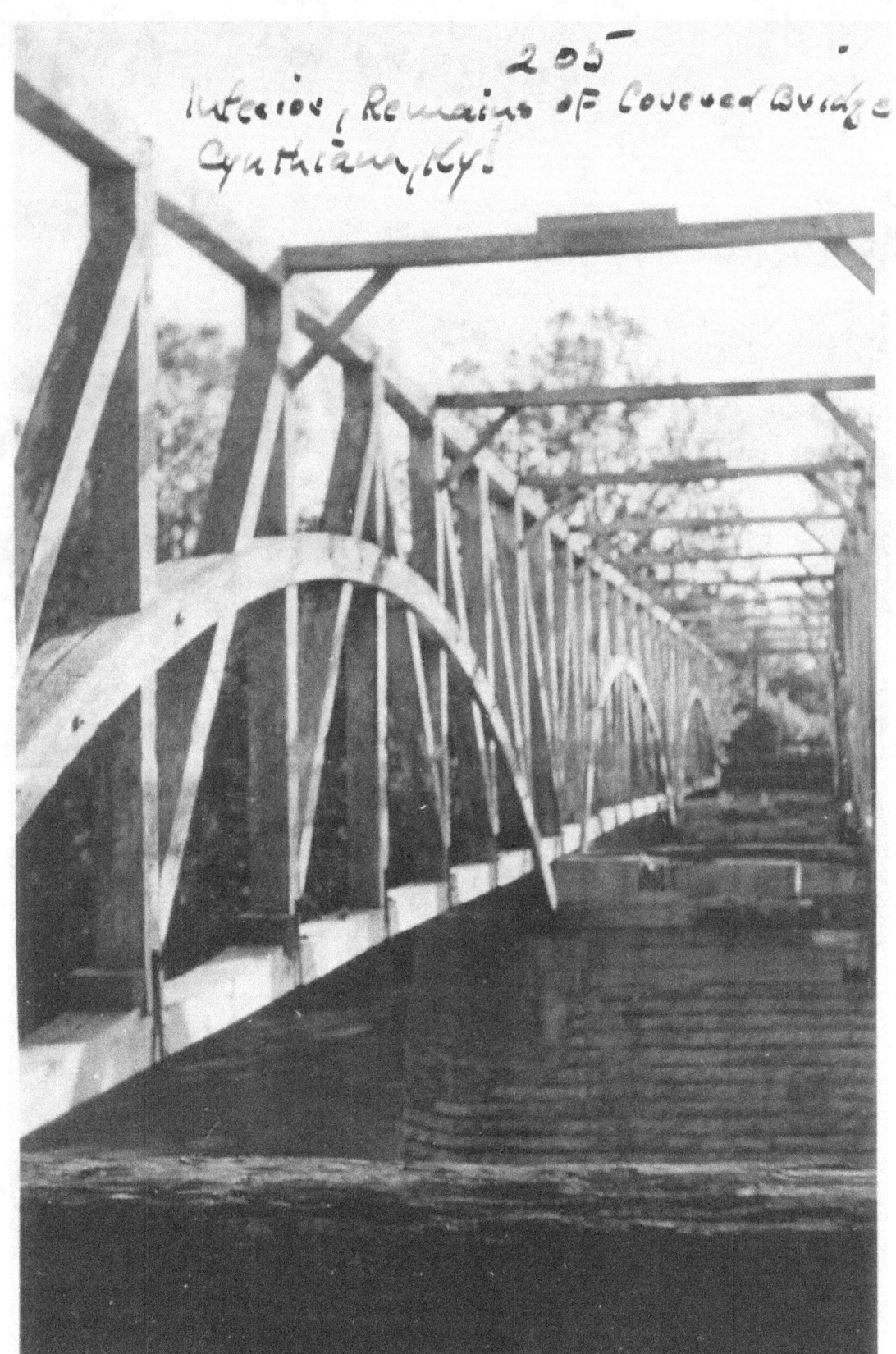

205
Interior, Remains of Covered Bridge
Cynthiana, Ky.

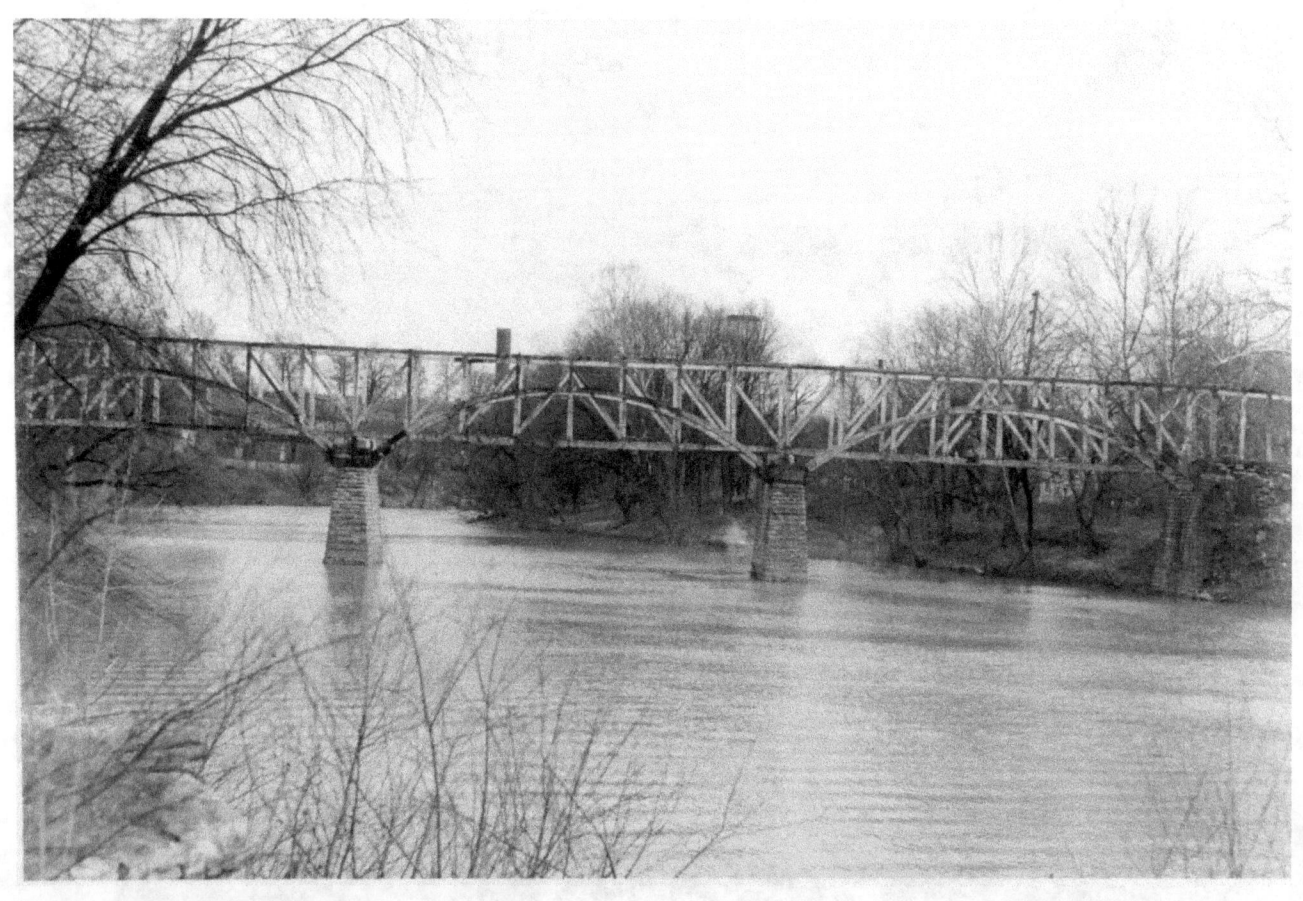

As the bridge was dismantled the usable timbers were salvaged to be reused for other projects in the county, including a barn. The skeleton of the bridge was sold but no way was found to remove the heavy timbers. In late December 1948 the remaining skeleton of the bridge was pushed into the river and this landmark was lost forever.

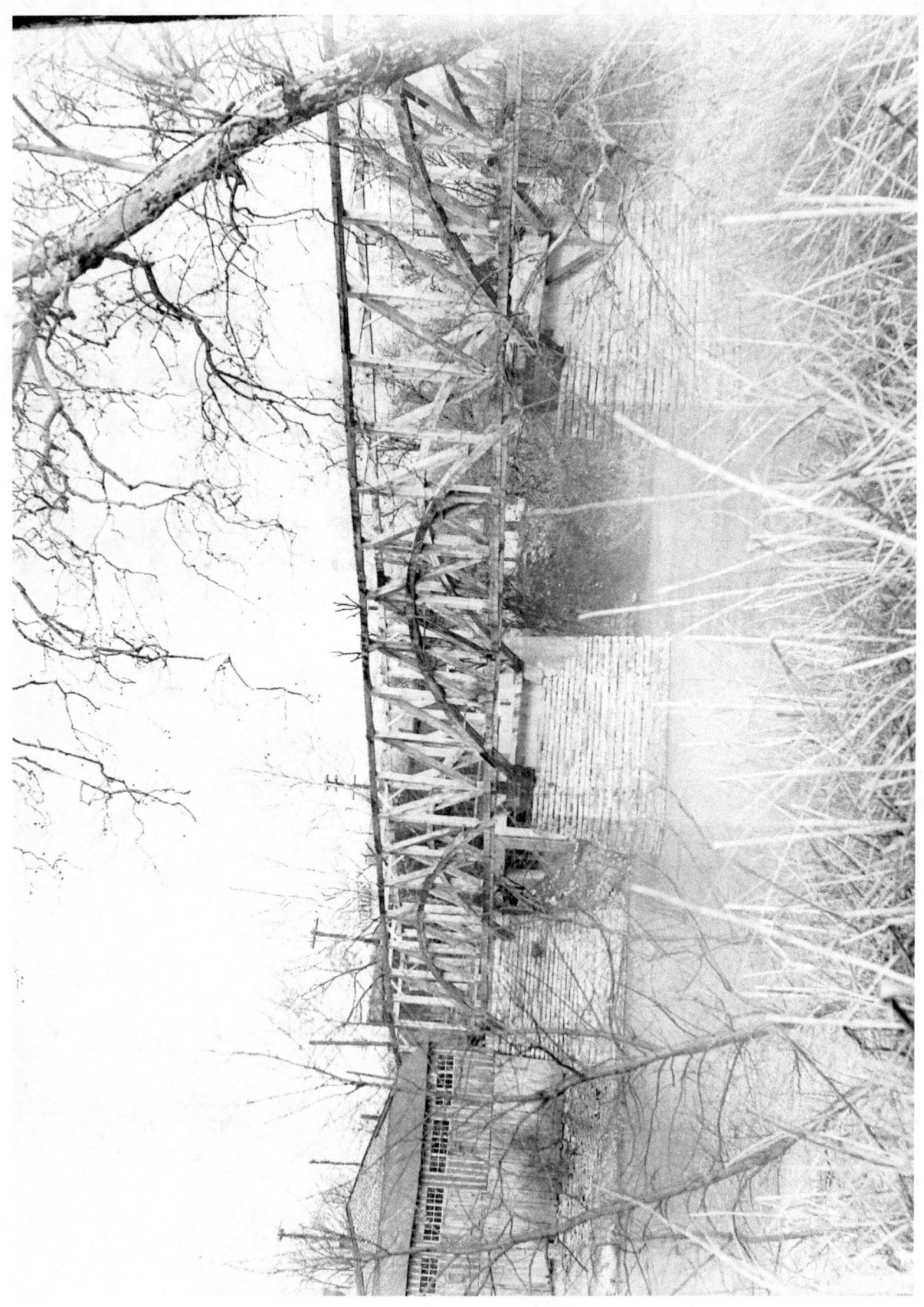

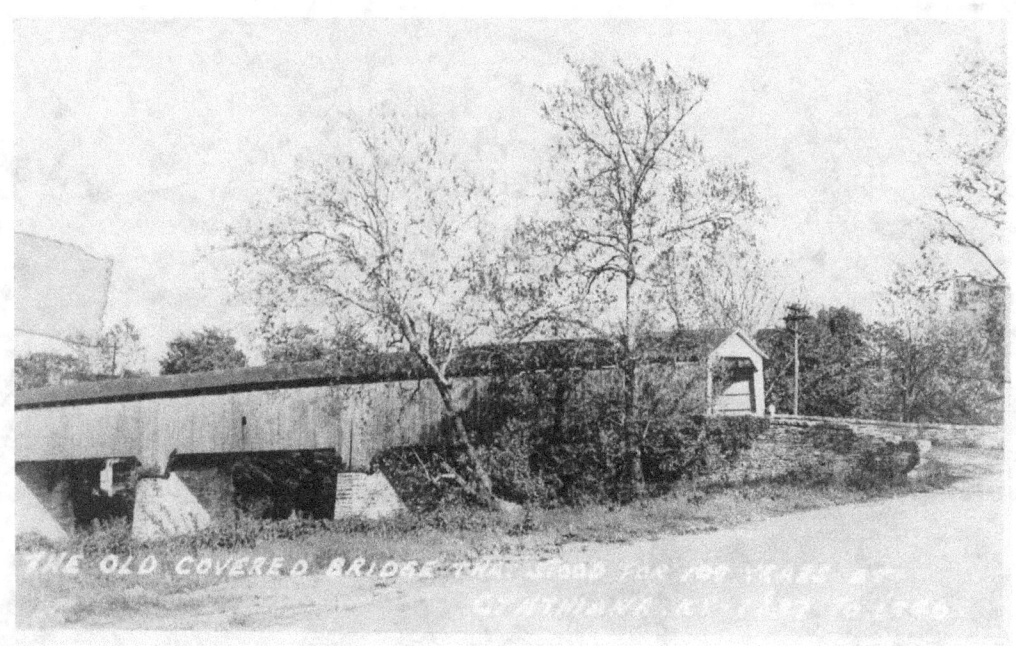

This postcard from the Cynthiana Businessman's Club is a good example of how the bridge remained popular even after its demolition. A Mrs. Van Buren from Long Island, New York had written for a souvenir postcard of the bridge produced by the club.

The last reaming trace of the bridge was removed in the winter of 1949 to make way for the new concrete bridge, which stands today. Here you can see a crane removing the wing walls and abutments.

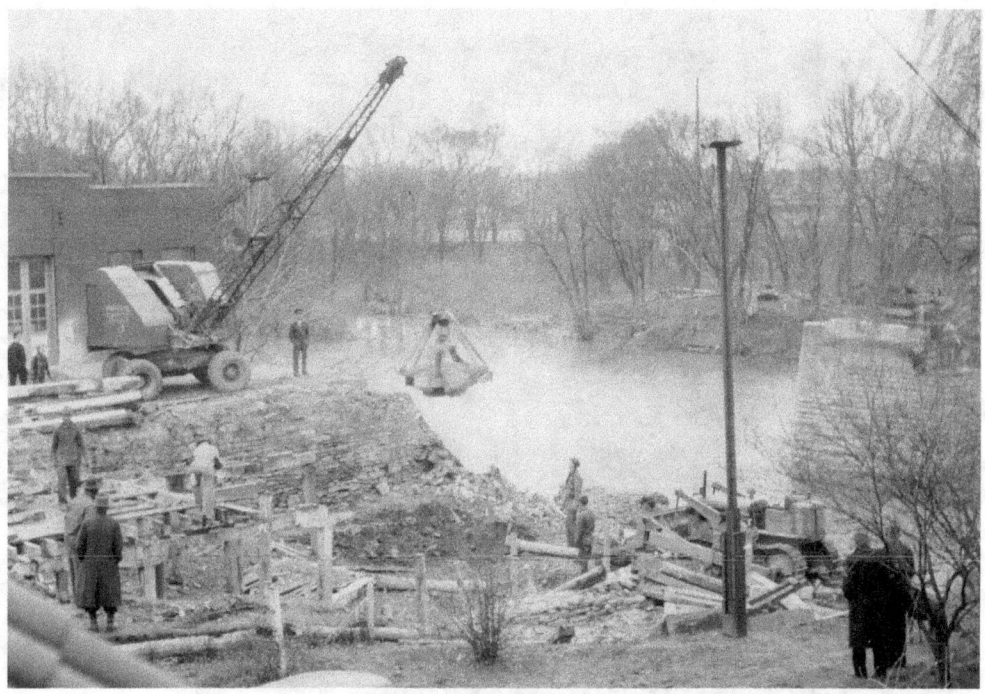

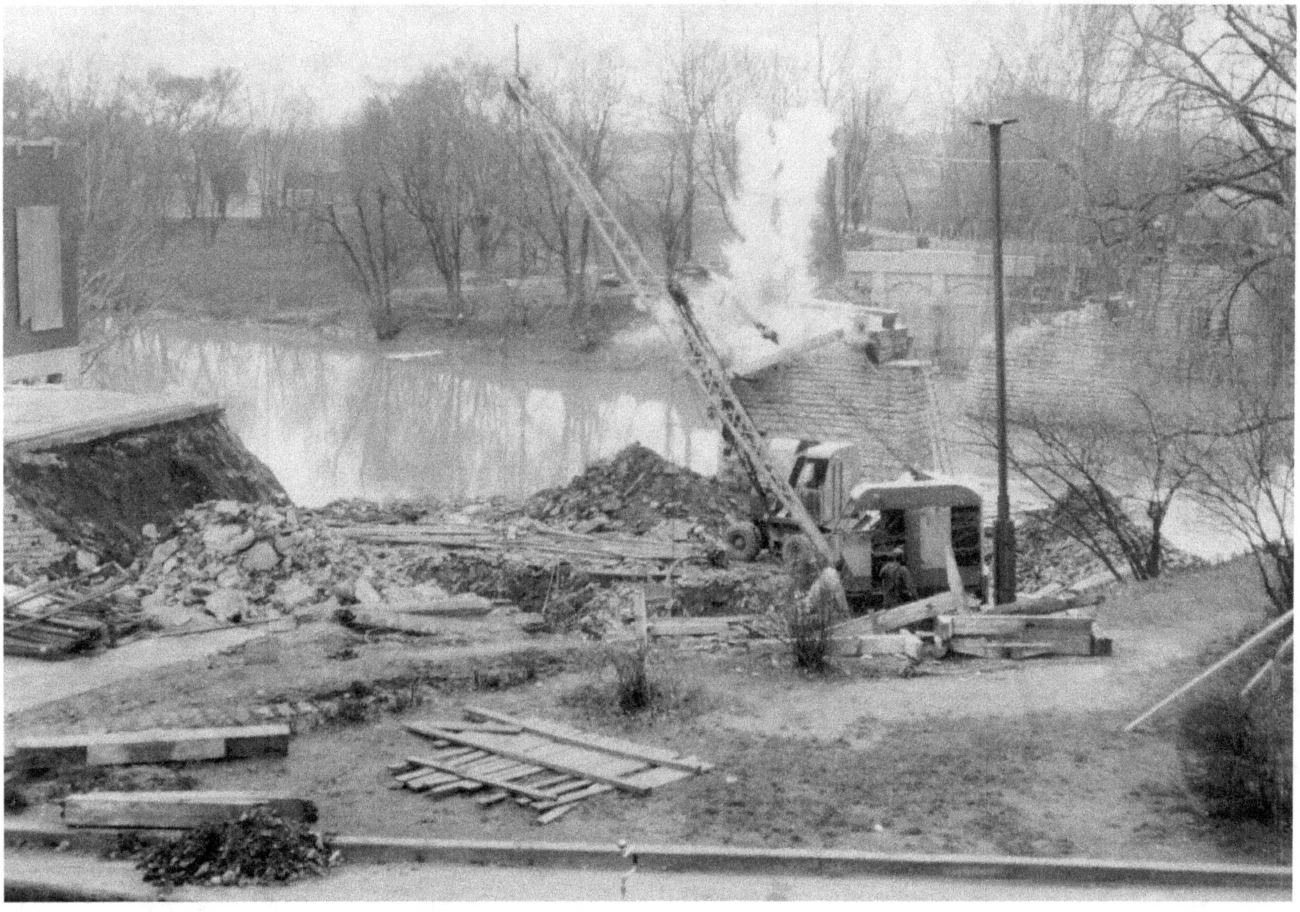

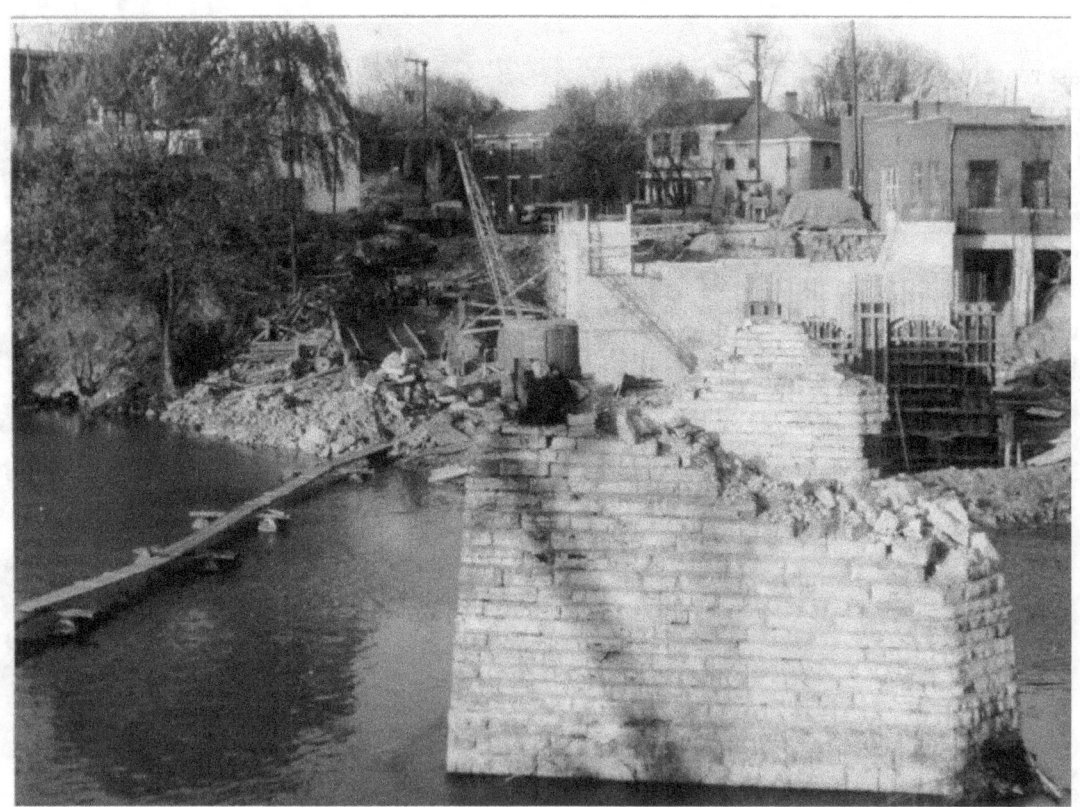

A portion of the bridge experienced a new life after the destruction of the bridge. Milton Criswell salvaged many of the timbers and constructed a barn on his farm on Old Curry Road in Harrison County. His son, Floyd, recalled building the barn with his father and brother, saying that they would inspect the bridge timbers and remove the nails with an ice pick so they would not break the saw blade. He also remembers during bad storms moving their livestock into the barn and sleeping in the hay loft until the storm passed. The barn stood until 2008 when it was damaged in a windstorm and the current owner of the property demolished the barn rather than repairing it.

Gray's Run

The covered bridge over Gray's Run stood only a half mile from Cynthiana's main covered bridge. The history of the bridge is not clear because some say the roof and sides were removed from the bridge in the 1920's and it was used "uncovered" until replaced with an iron bridge.

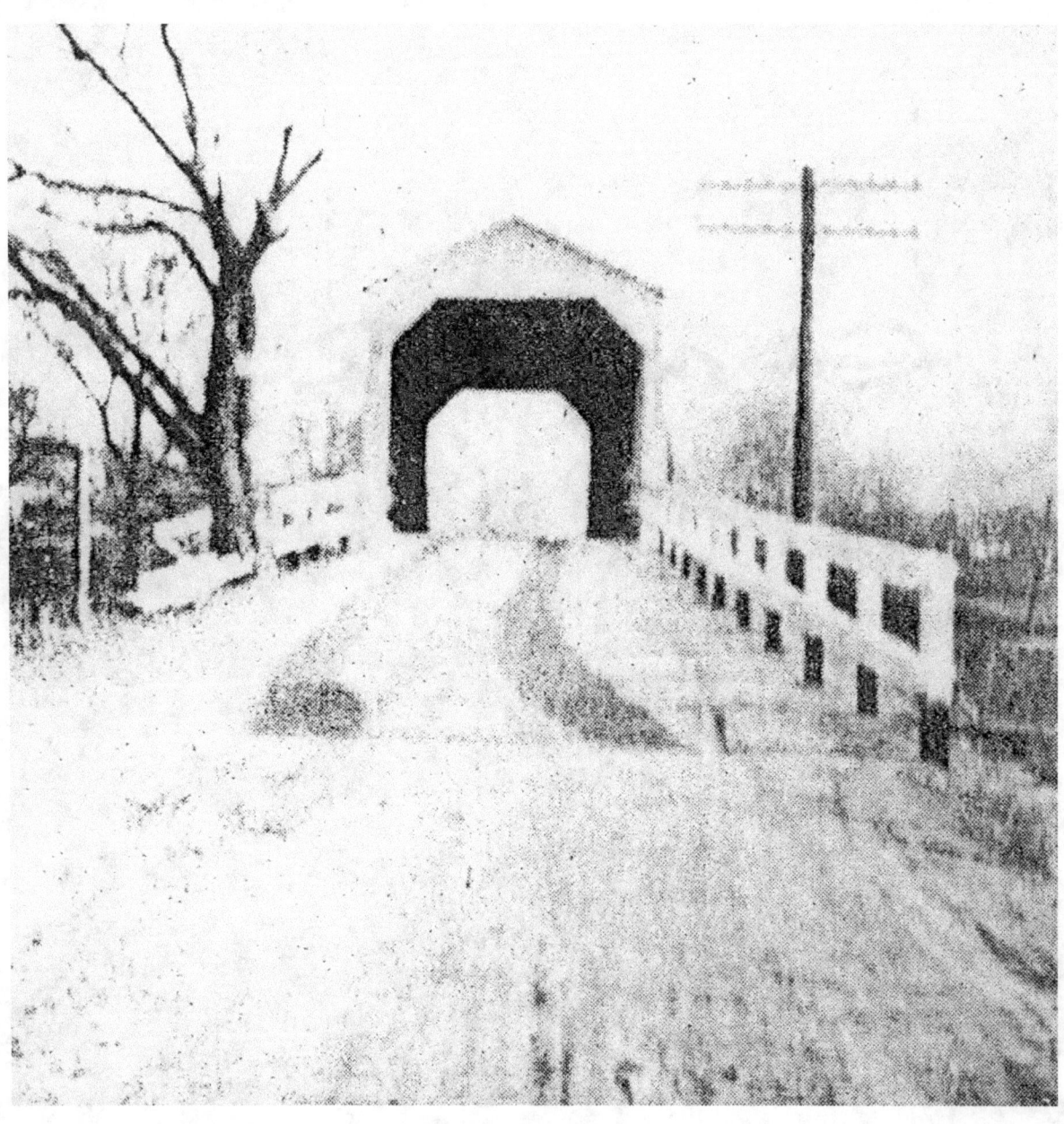

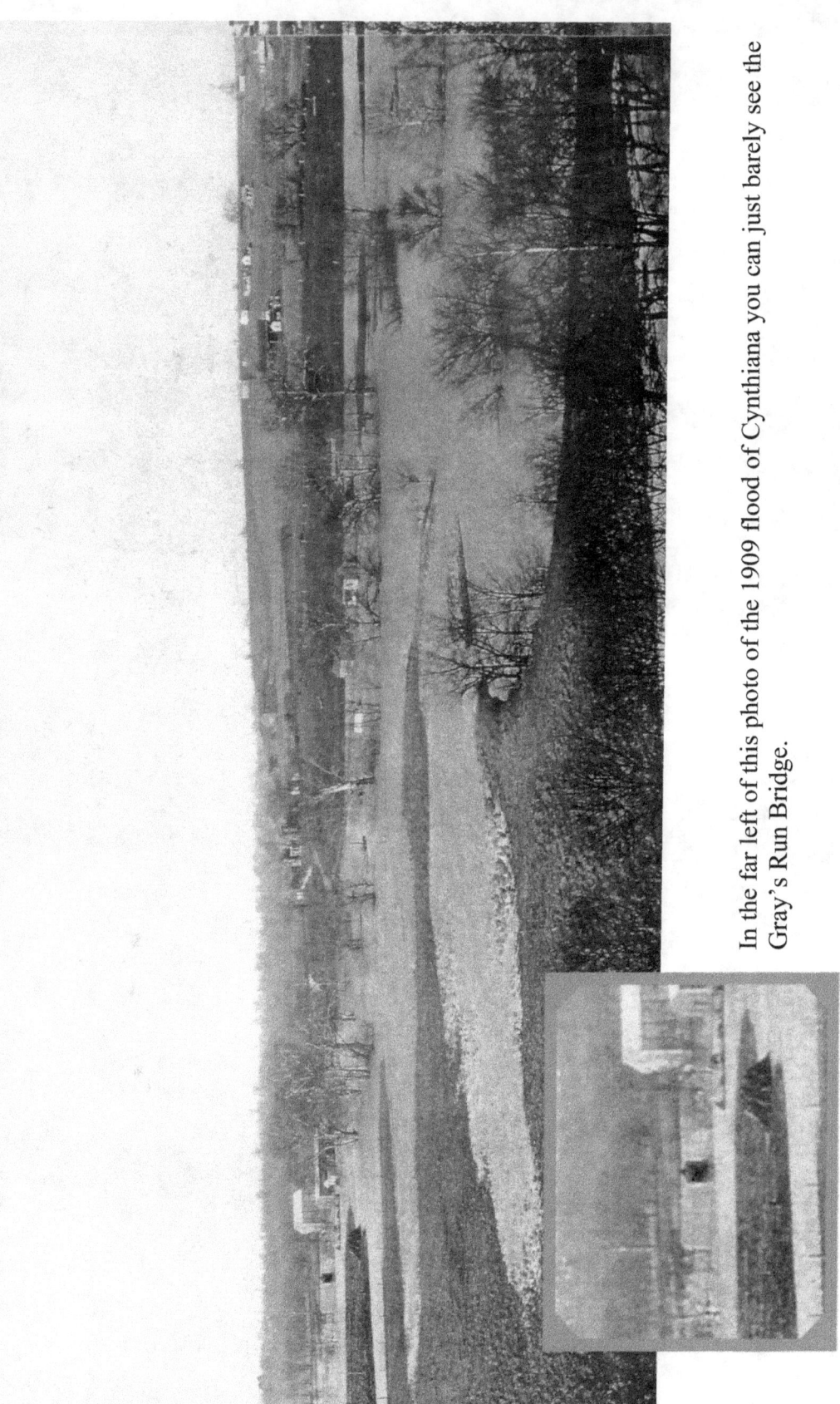

In the far left of this photo of the 1909 flood of Cynthiana you can just barely see the Gray's Run Bridge.

83

Lair Station

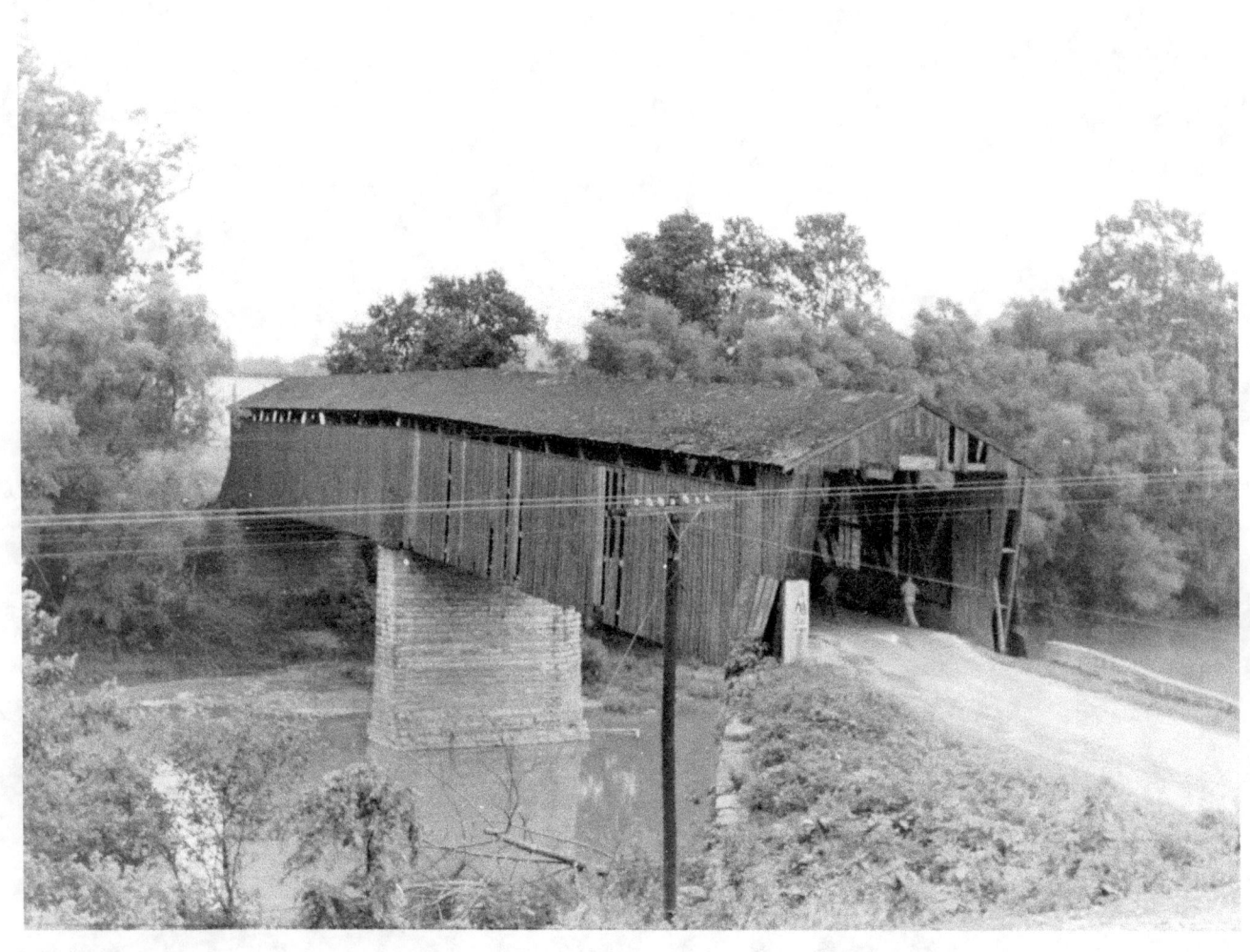

The Lair Station Bridge was constructed in 1871 by John and Matthias Lair.

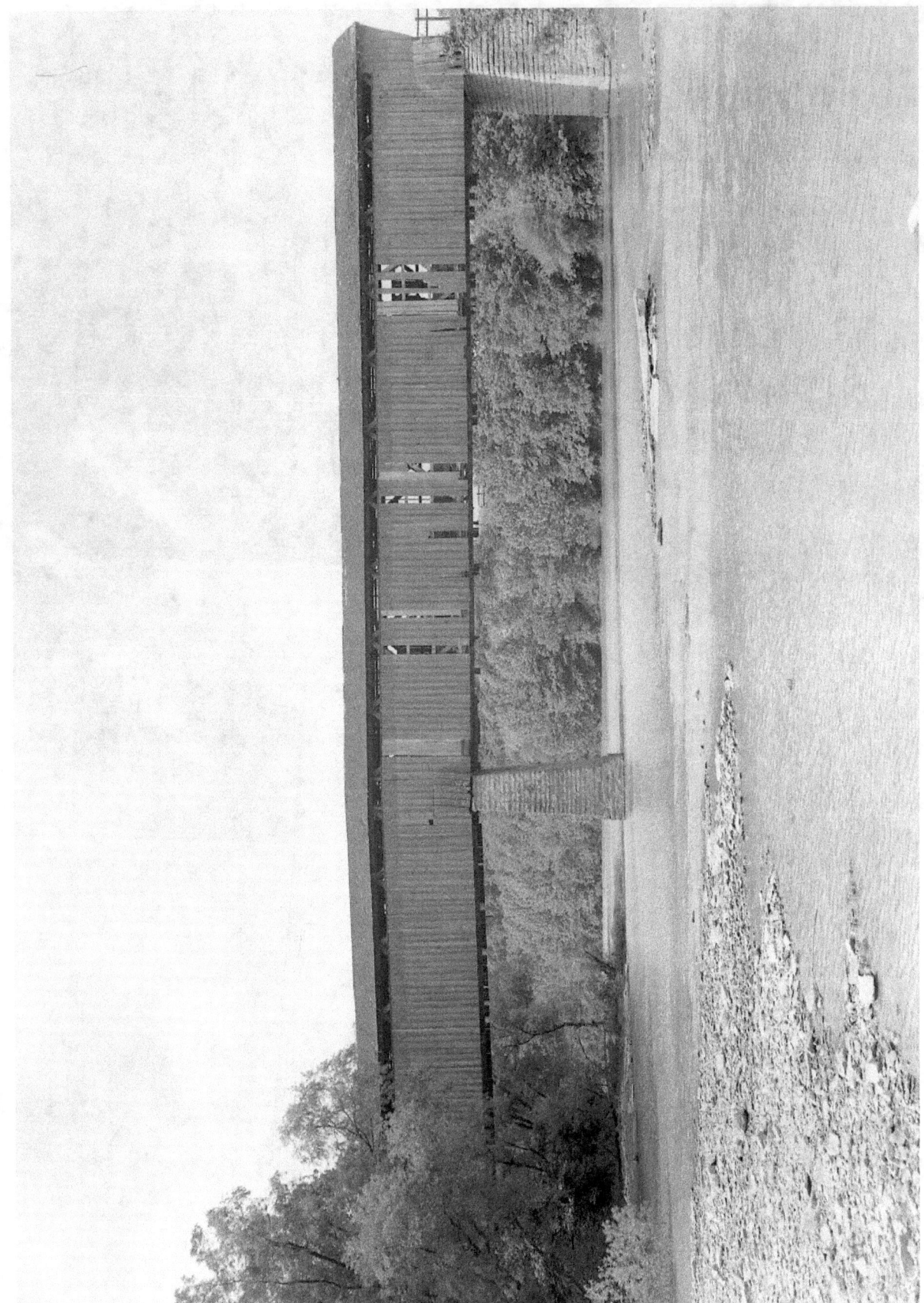

The 270 foot Howe Truss bridge stood approximately 30 feet above the South Fork of the Licking River.

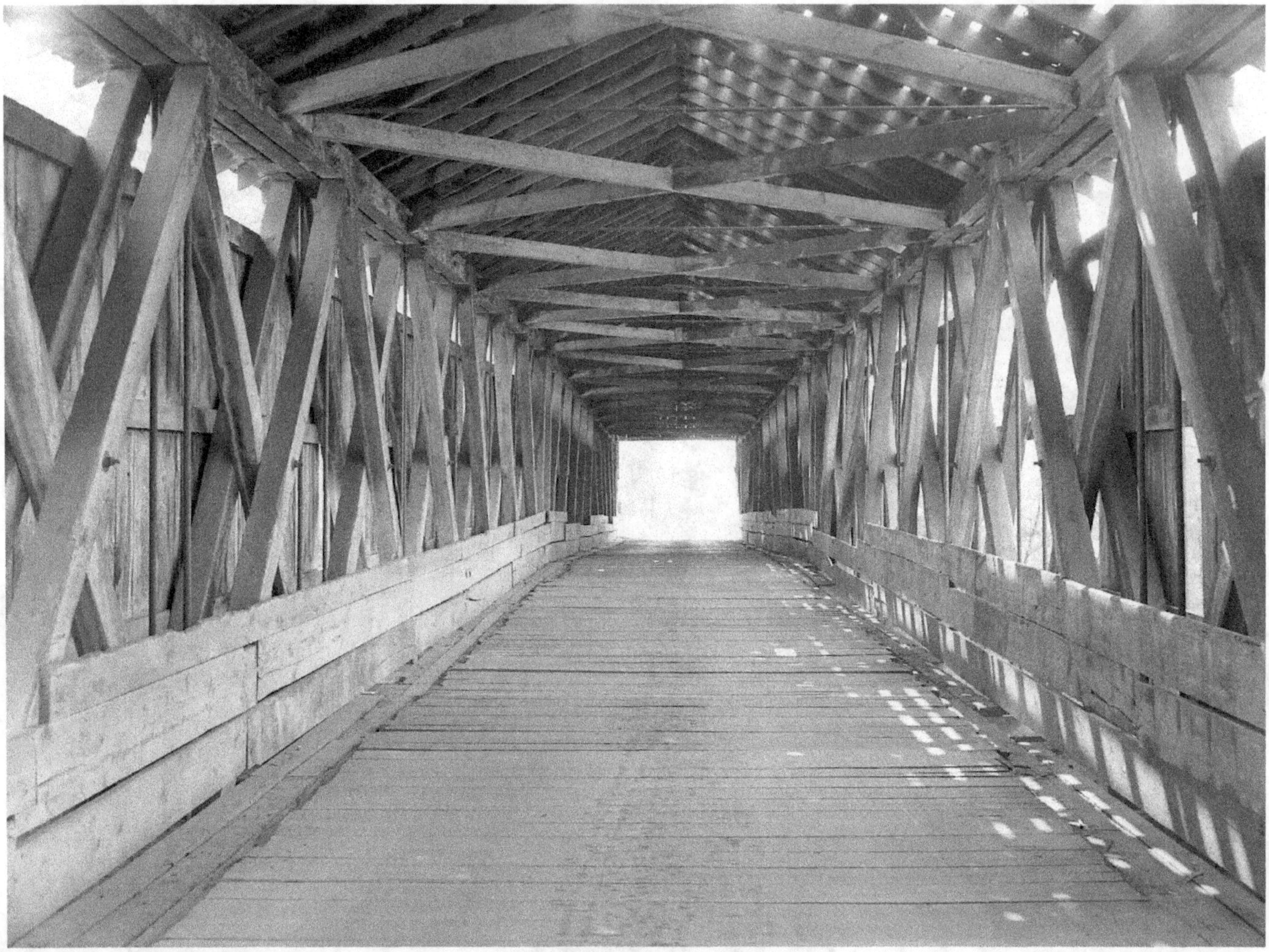

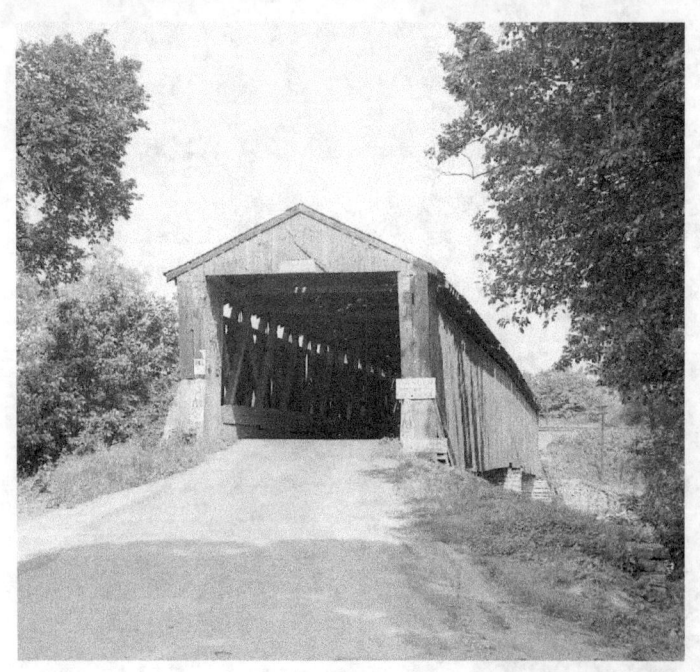

May 30, 1942

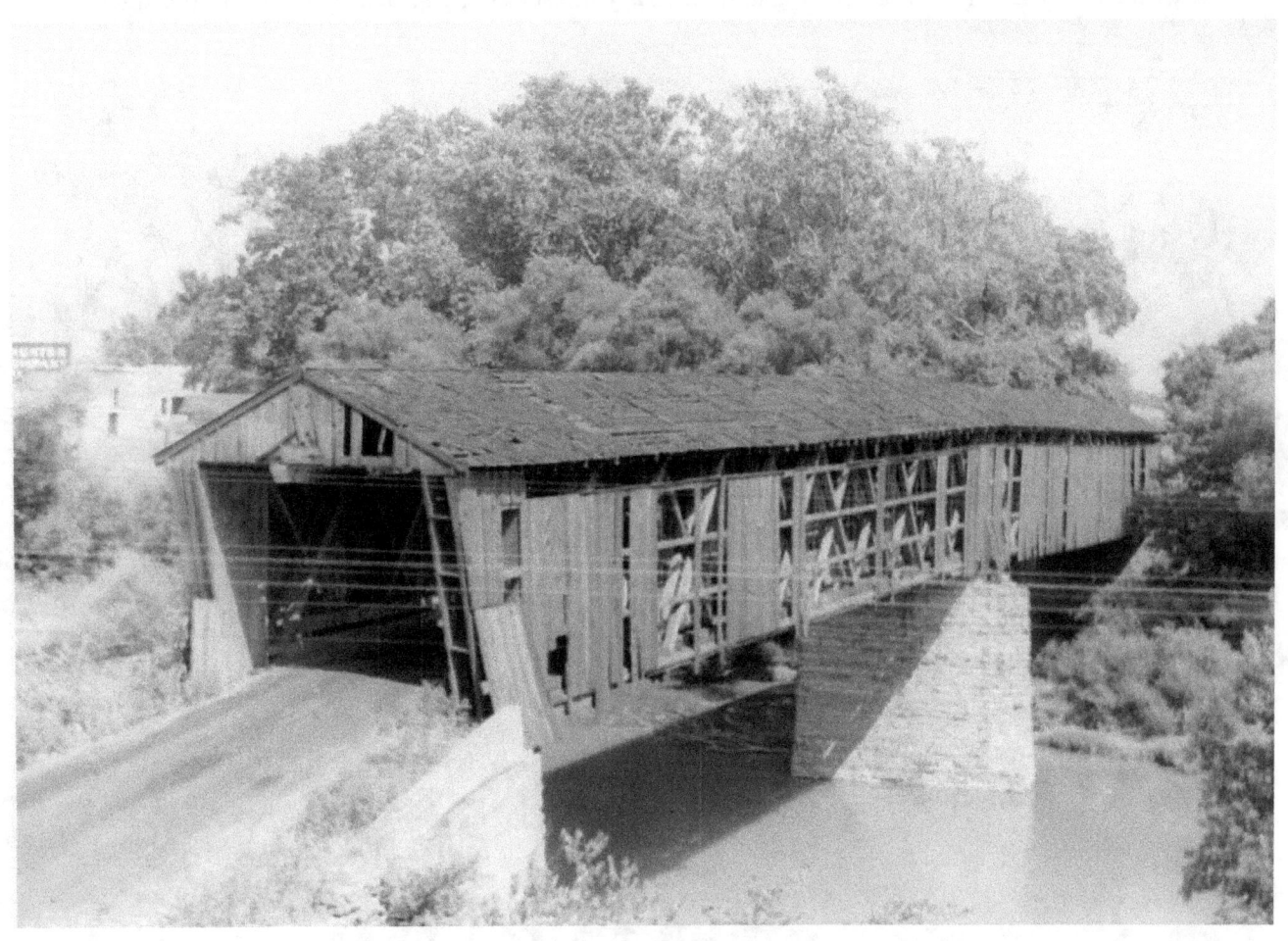

The Lair Station Bridge is perhaps the most dramatic example of a neglected covered bridge. After receiving a phone call from a Lair resident on July 11, 1946 stating that the bridge was making a strange "ticking" sound after large trucks crossed it, County Judge Executive W.E. Boswell and County Engineer Harvey Criswell inspected the bridge. They concluded that although it looked "ok" outwardly, they ultimately condemned it and closed it to traffic because of the resident's concerns until it could be inspected more thoroughly.

Thirty minutes after condemnation, the north span collapsed into the river. Several local boys were beneath the bridge fishing and narrowly missed being struck by the falling bridge.

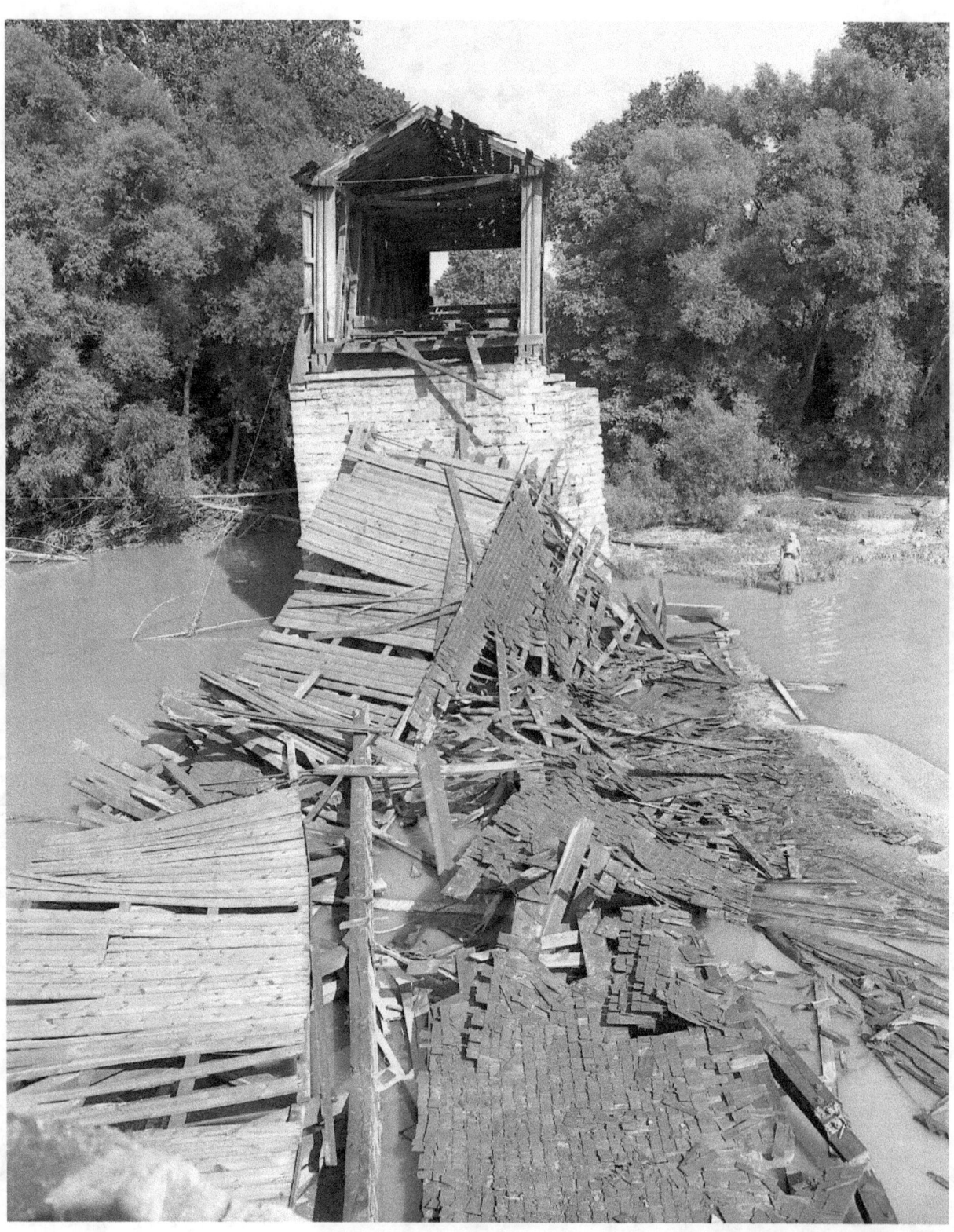

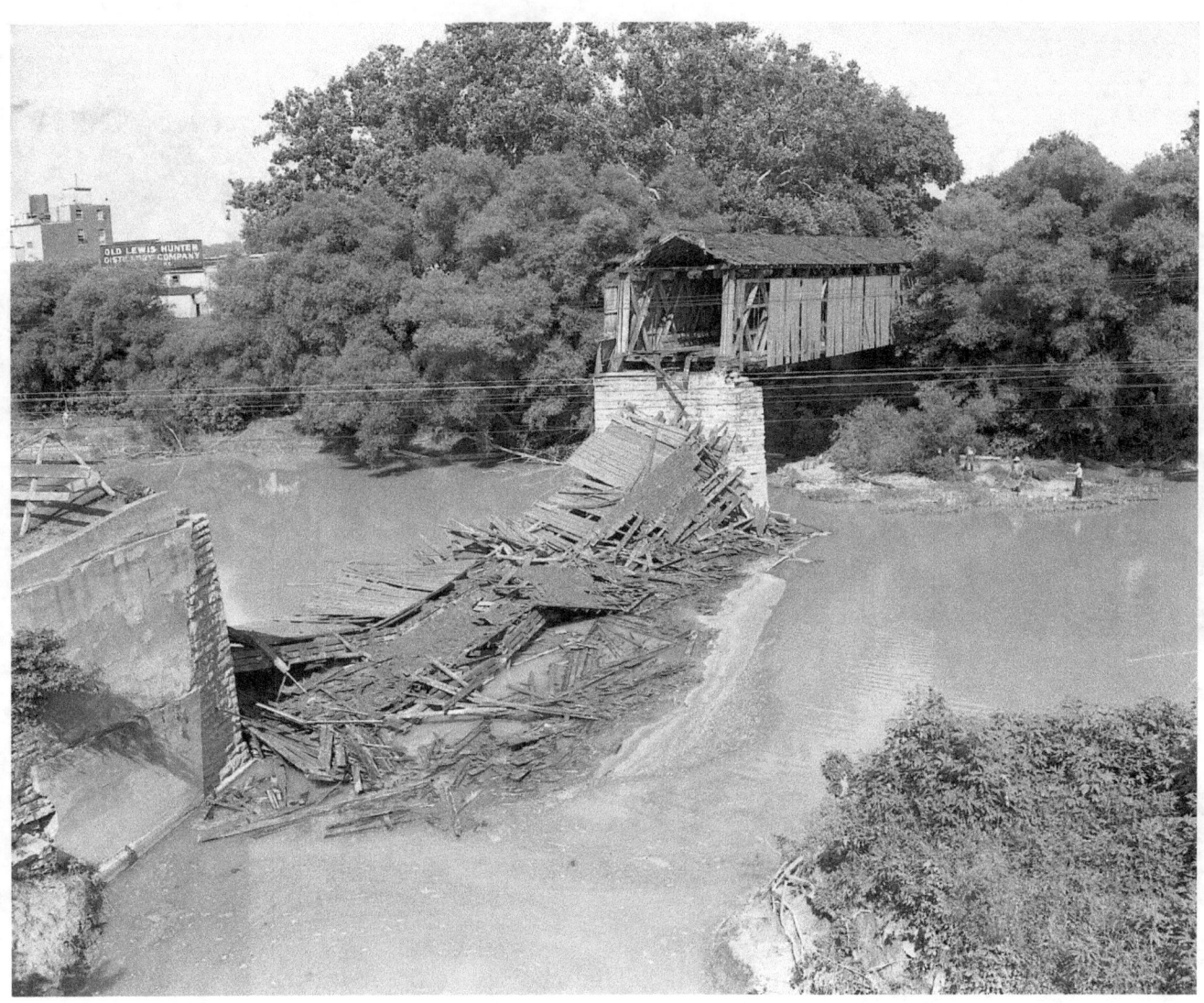

July 14, 1946

After the collapse the county was faced with the dilemma of either repairing the bridge or building a new one. The nearby Lewis Hunter Distillery (seen in the upper left of the photo) was adding to the pressure because they faced double hauling charges and may have been forced to shut down temporarily until a solution was found. One possibility being considered was re-using shorter steel spans that were removed from other areas of the state.

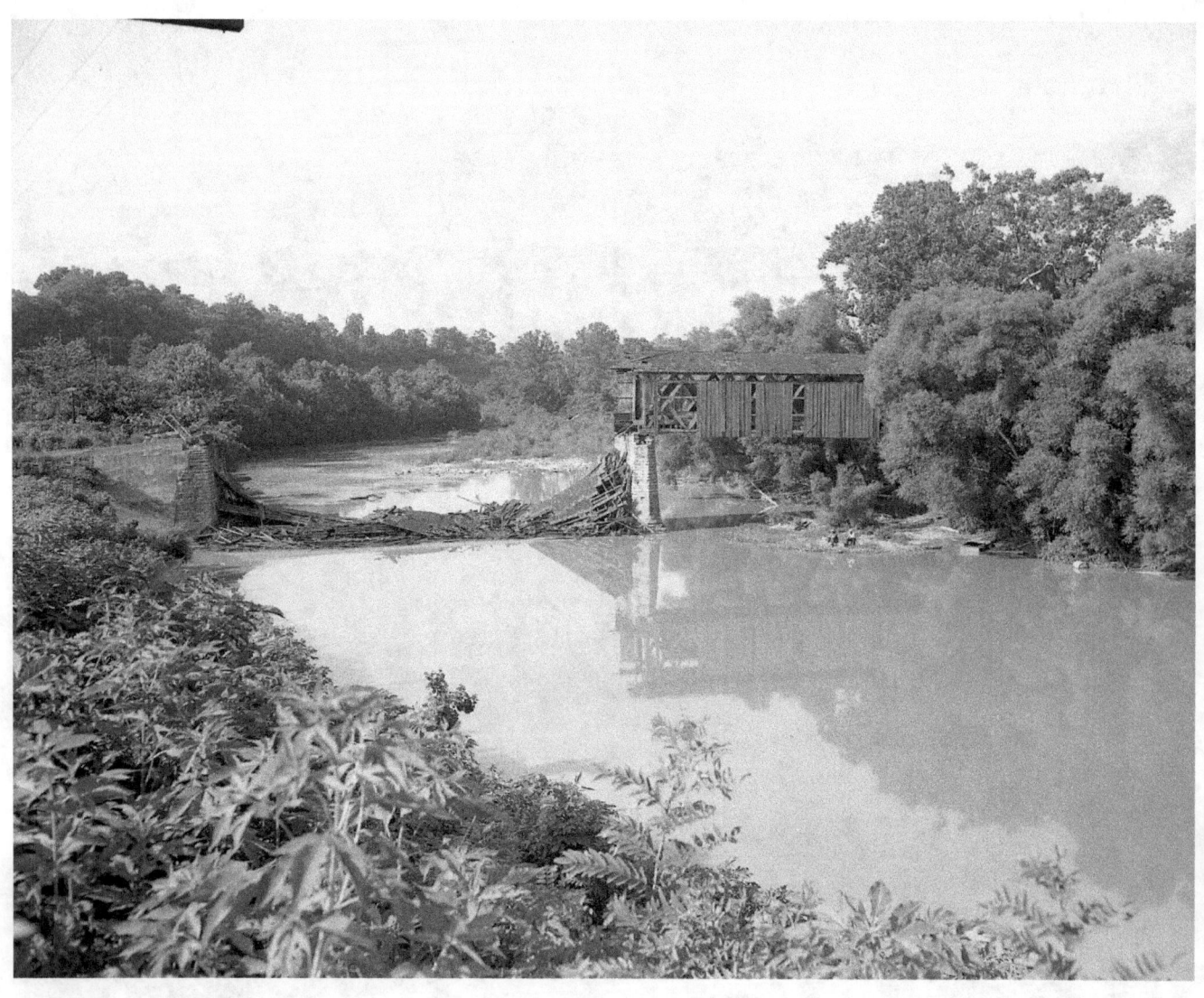

To add insult to injury, five nights after the bridge's collapse a fire destroyed the section of the bridge that was in the river burned, possibly due to a carelessly tossed cigarette. The burned timbers could not be salvaged and the decision was made to replace the entire bridge with a concrete one.

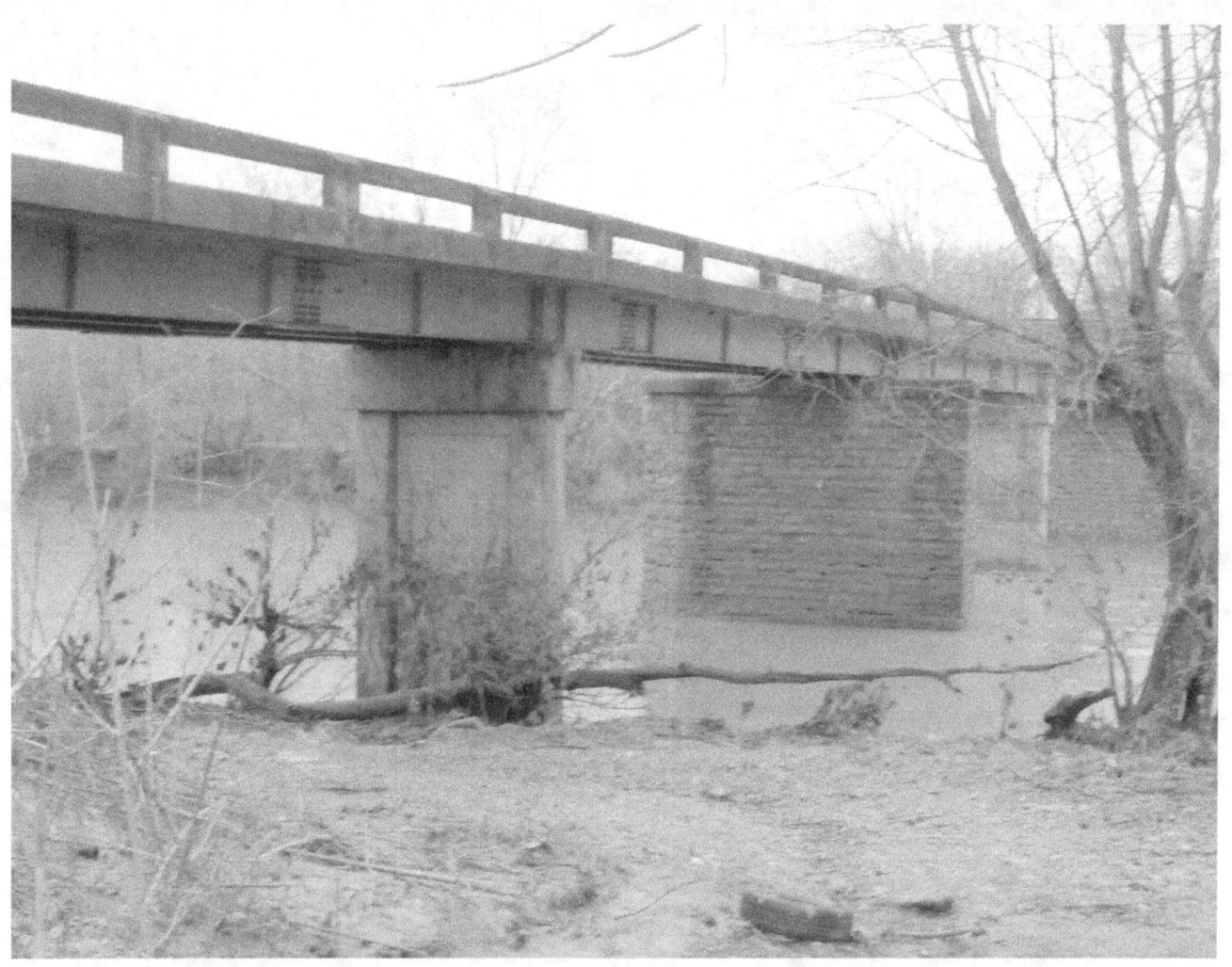

To date, the replacement one-lane concrete bridge utilizes the old stone abutments and stone center pier that once supported the covered bridge.

February 23, 2019

About the Author

Melissa C. Jurgensen is the author of several books, including *River Towns of Central Kentucky* and *Covered Bridges of Bourbon County, Kentucky*. Melissa was awarded the commission of Kentucky Colonel in 2006, the highest honor in the Commonwealth, due to her advocacy for the restoration and preservation of Kentucky's covered bridges. Melissa also serves on the board of the Harrodsburg Historical Society, and as an Executive Bourbon Steward, she has a keen interest in the history and evolution of Kentucky's all important bourbon industry.

Photo Credits

Collection of French Patterson: 13 (top), 14, 15, 31, 34, 76 and 77

Collection of William Penn: 53 (top) and 83.

Collection of Cynthiana-Harrison County Museum: Cover, 35 (bottom) and 82.

Collection of Philip Naff: 51 (top) and 53 (bottom).

Cordelia Hart McKinney Collection: 10, 20, 21, 22, 23, 24, 25, 26 and 27.

Taugott Keller Collection: 12.

Sharon Dennis Fowler Collection: 55 (bottom).

Titles by Melissa Jurgensen

High Bridge, Kentucky

Through their Eyes: Covered Bridges of Bourbon County, Kentucky

Through their Eyes: Covered Bridges of Harrison County, Kentucky

Through their Eyes: Covered Bridges of Fleming County, Kentucky

Through their Eyes: Covered Bridges of Franklin County, Kentucky

River Towns of Central Kentucky

Kentucky's Covered Bridges (with Laughlin)